UKULELE

MORE SIMPLE SONGS

The Easiest Tunes to Strum & Sing on Ukulele

ISBN 978-1-5400-2743-6

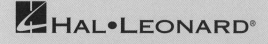

HAL•LEONARD®

Visit Hal Leonard Online at
www.halleonard.com

Contact Us:
Hal Leonard
7777 West Bluemound Road
Milwaukee, WI 53213
Email: info@halleonard.com

In Europe contact:
Hal Leonard Europe Limited
42 Wigmore Street
Marylebone, London, W1U 2RN
Email: info@halleonardeurope.com

In Australia contact:
Hal Leonard Australia Pty. Ltd.
4 Lentara Court
Cheltenham, Victoria, 3192 Australia
Email: info@halleonard.com.au

CONTENTS

Another Day in Paradise

Words and Music by Phil Collins

First note

Verse
Steadily

1. She calls out ___ to the man ___ on the street, ___
2. He walks on, ___   does-n't look back. ___
3. She calls out ___ to the man ___ on the street, ___
4. You can tell ___ from the lines ___ on her face, ___

"Sir, ___ can you help ___ me?"   "It's cold ___ and I've no -
He pre - tends ___ he can't hear ___ her.   Starts to whis - tle as he
he can see ___ she's been cry - ing.   She's got blis - ters on the
you can see ___ that she's been ___ there.   Prob - a - bly been moved on from

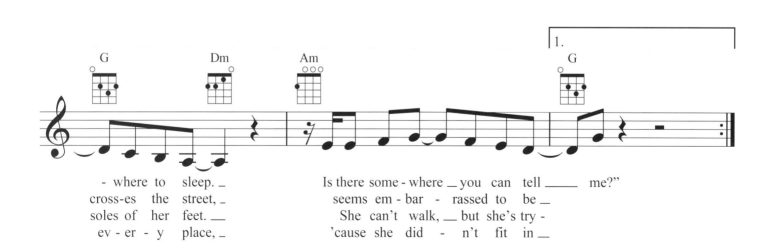

1.

- where to sleep. ___   Is there some - where ___ you can tell ___ me?"
cross - es the street, ___   seems em - bar - rassed to be ___
soles of her feet. ___   She can't walk, ___ but she's try -
ev - er - y place, ___   'cause she did - n't fit in ___

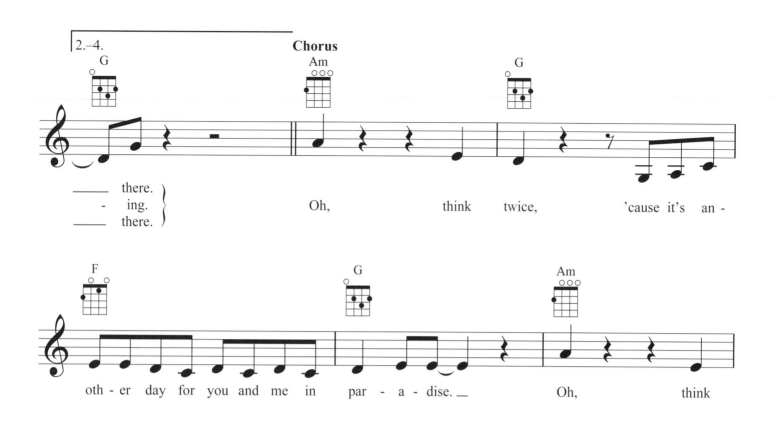

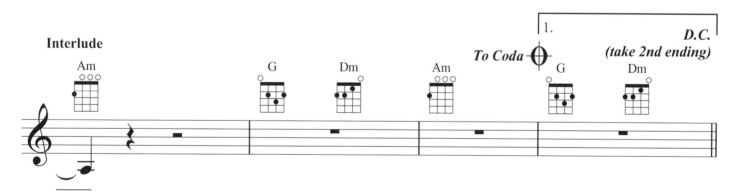

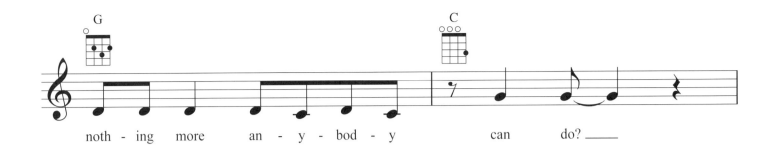

noth - ing more an - y - bod - y can do? ____

Oh, _____ Lord, ____ there must be

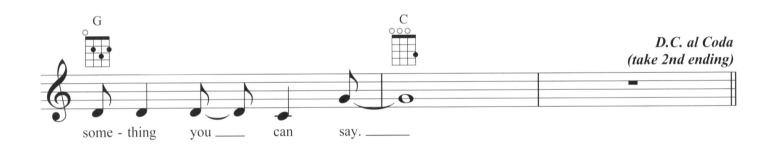

D.C. al Coda
(take 2nd ending)

some - thing you ____ can say. ____

Coda

Outro

It's just an - oth - er day ____ for

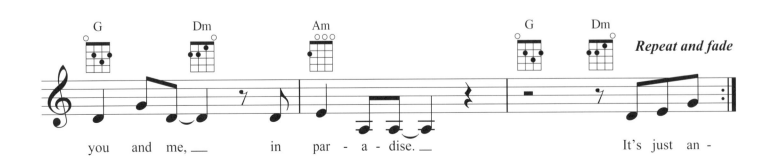

Repeat and fade

you and me, ____ in par - a - dise. ____ It's just an -

Come On Get Higher

Words and Music by Matt Nathanson and Mark Weinberg

Chorus

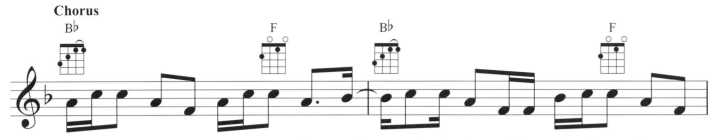

come on, get high-er, loos-en my lips. Faith ___ and de-sire and the swing of your hips. Just

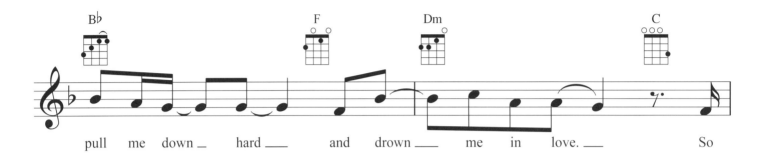

pull me down ___ hard ___ and drown ___ me in love. ___ So

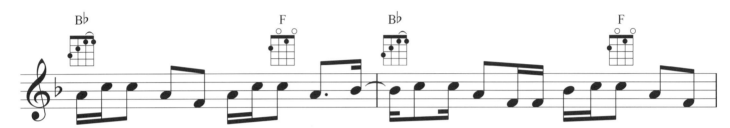

come on, get high-er, loos-en my lips. Faith ___ and de-sire and the swing of your hips. Just

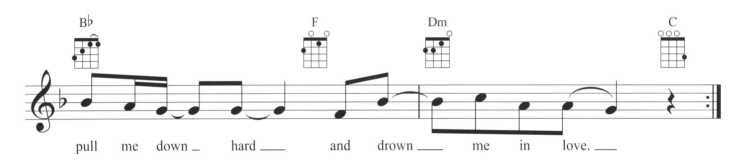

pull me down ___ hard ___ and drown ___ me in love. ___

Bridge

I miss the pull of your ___ heart, I taste the sparks on your tongue.

I see an-gels and dev-ils and God ___ when you come ___ on, ___ hold ___

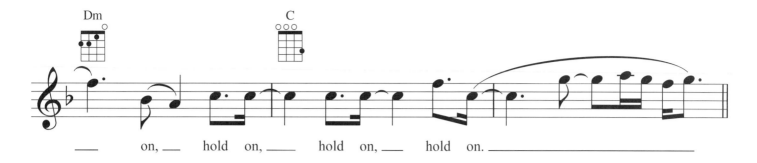

___ on, ___ hold on, ___ hold on, ___ hold on. _____

Outro-Chorus

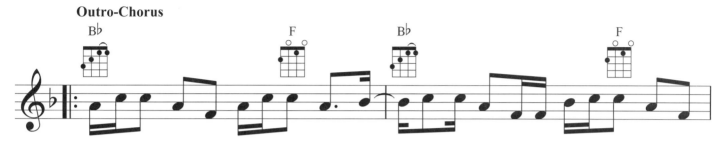

Come on, get high - er, loos-en my lips. Faith ___ and de-sire and the swing of your hips. Just

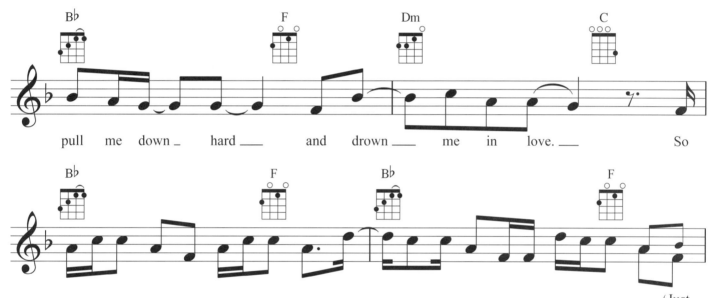

pull me down ___ hard ___ and drown ___ me in love. ___ So

come on, get high - er, loos-en my lips. Faith ___ and de-sire and the swing of your hips. {Just {Ev -

1.

pull me down ___ hard ___ and drown ___ me, drown ___ me in love.

2.

'ry-thing works, ___ love, ev - 'ry-thing works ___ in your ___ arms.

Be-Bop-A-Lula

Words and Music by Tex Davis and Gene Vincent

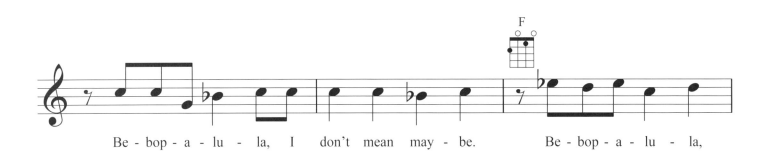

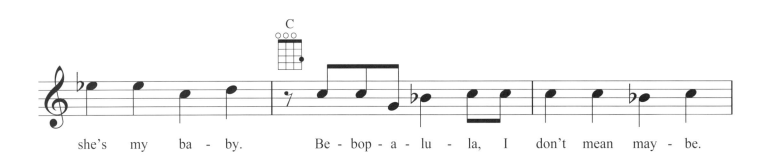

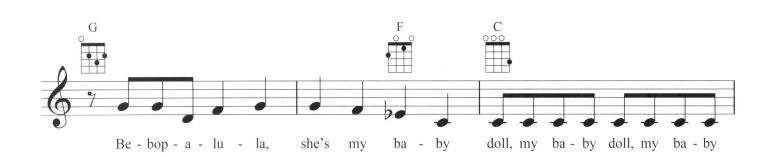

Blue Eyes Crying in the Rain

Words and Music by Fred Rose

First note

Verse
Sadly, in 2

1. In the twi - light glow I see her, _____
2. Now my hair has turned to sil - ver. _____

blue eyes cry - ing in the rain. _____
All my life I've loved in vain. _____

As we kissed good - bye and part - ed, _____
I can see her star in heav - en, _____

_____ I knew we'd nev - er meet a -
_____ blue eyes cry - ing in the

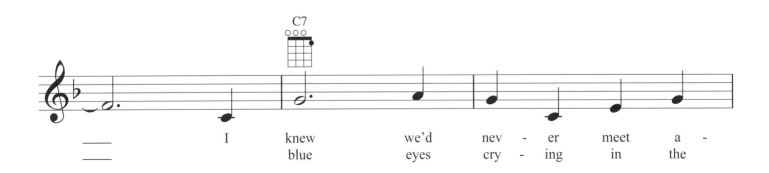

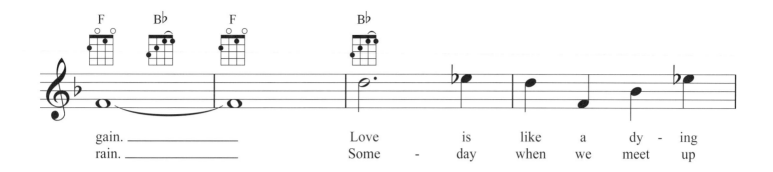

gain. _____

rain. _____ Love is like a dy - ing

Some - day when we meet up

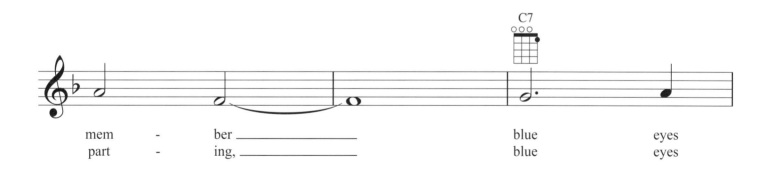

em - ber, _____ on - ly mem - o - ries re -

yon - der, _____ we'll stroll hand in hand a -

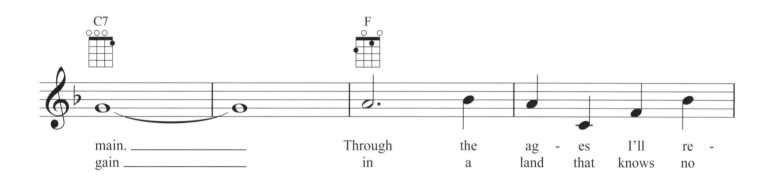

main. _____ Through the ag - es I'll re -

gain _____ in a land that knows no

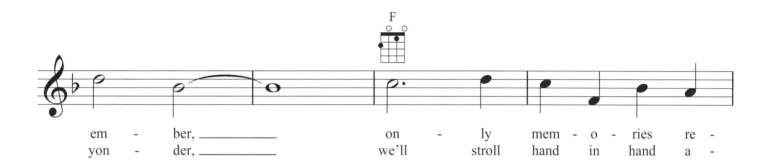

mem - ber _____ blue eyes

part - ing, _____ blue eyes

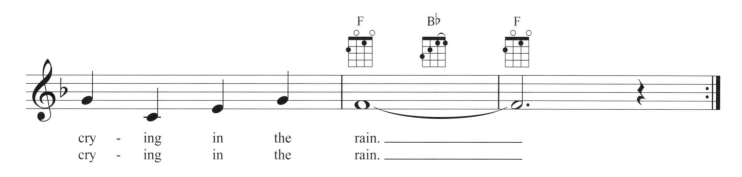

cry - ing in the rain. _____

cry - ing in the rain. _____

Budapest

Words and Music by George Barnett and Joel Pott

First note

Verse
Moderately fast

1. My house in Bu - da - pest; my, _____ my hid - den treas - ure chest; _

gold - en grand pi - an - o; _____ my beau - ti - ful cas - til - lo: you, ooh, _

you, ooh, _ I'd leave it all.

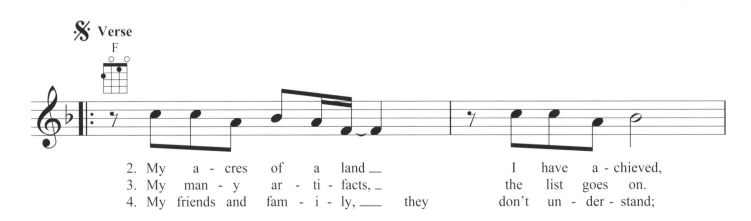

2. My a - cres of a land _ I have a - chieved,
3. My man - y ar - ti - facts, _ the list goes on.
4. My friends and fam - i - ly, _ they don't un - der - stand;

it may be hard for you to _____ stop and be - lieve. _____ But for
If you just say the words, I, _____ I'll up and run. _____ Oh, to
they feel they'll lose so much if _____ you take my hand. _____ But for

you, ooh, _____ you, ooh, _____ I'd leave it all.   Oh, for
you, ooh, _____ you, ooh, _____ I'd leave it all.   Oh, to
you, ooh, _____ you, ooh, _____ I'd lose it all.   Oh, for

you, ooh, _____ you, ooh, _____ I'd leave it all.
you, ooh, _____ you, ooh, _____ I'd leave it all.
you, ooh, _____ you, ooh, _____ I'd lose it all.

Chorus

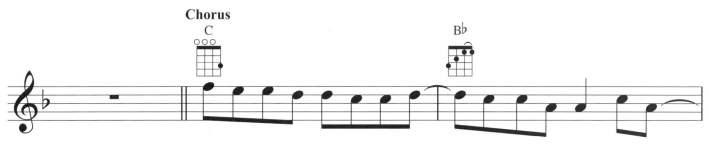

Give me one good rea - son why I _____ should nev - er make a change. _____

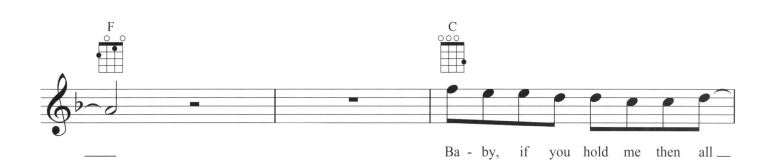

_____   Ba - by, if you hold me then all _____

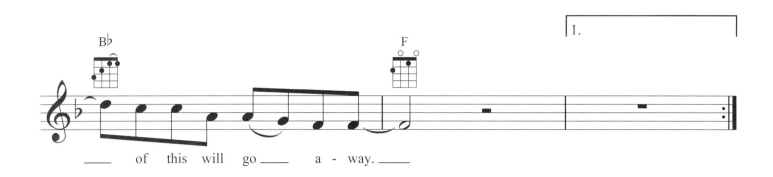

_ of this will go _ a - way. _

Chorus

Give me one good rea - son why I _ should nev - er make a change. _

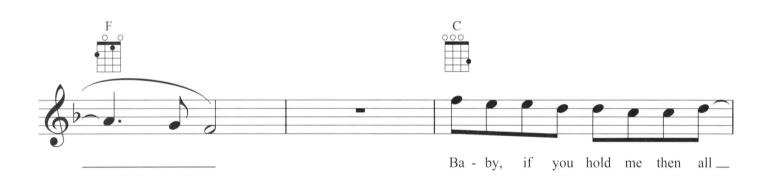

_ Ba - by, if you hold me then all _

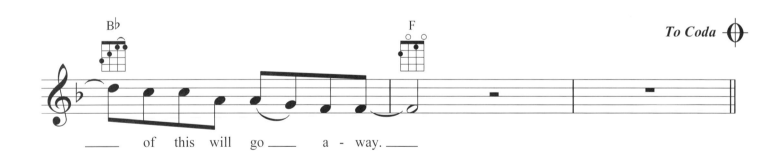

_ of this will go _ a - way. _

Interlude

(Instrumental)

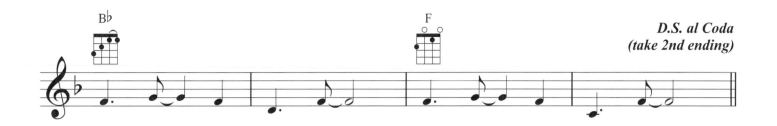

D.S. al Coda
(take 2nd ending)

Outro-Verse

My house in Bu - da - pest; my, ___ my hid - den treas - ure chest; ___

gold - en grand pi - an - o; ___ my beau - ti - ful cas - til - lo: you, ooh, ___

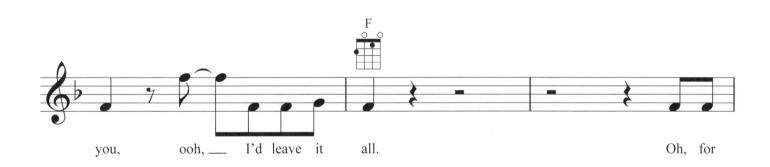

you, ooh, ___ I'd leave it all. Oh, for

you, ooh, ___ you, ooh, ___ I'd leave it all.

Coat of Many Colors

Words and Music by Dolly Parton

First note

Verse
Moderately, in 2

1. Back through the years __ I go wan-d'ring once a - gain, __

back __ to the sea - sons of __ my _____ youth. __ I re -

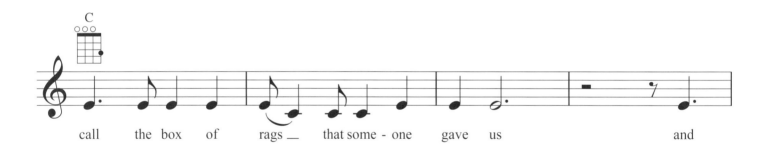

call the box of rags __ that some - one gave us and

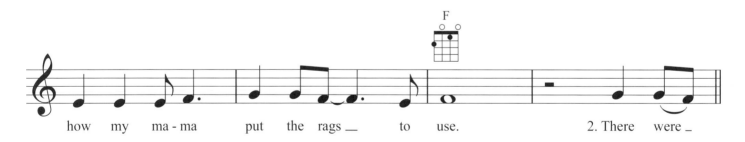

how my ma - ma put the rags __ to use. 2. There were __

rags of ____ man - y col - ors, ____ but ev - 'ry piece was small, and I

(3.–5.) *See additional lyrics*

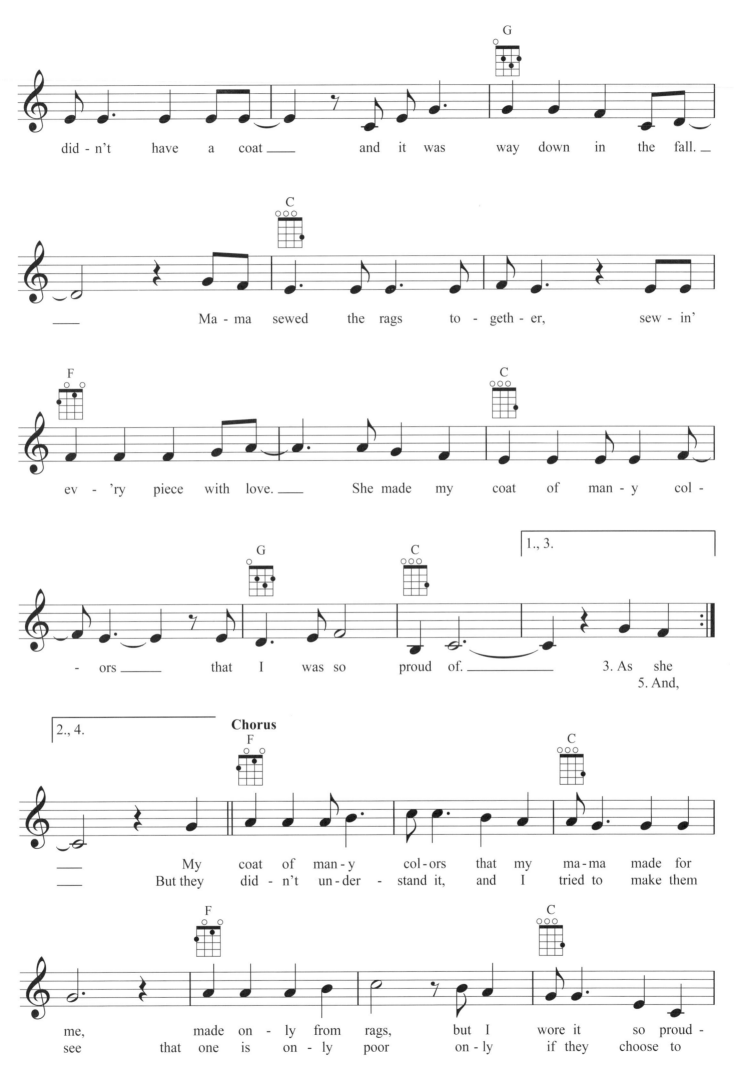

ly.

Al - though we had ___ no mon-ey, well, I was

be.

Now, I know we had ___ no mon-ey, but I was

rich as I ___ could be ___ in my coat of man - y

To Coda

D.S. al Coda
(with repeat)

col - ors ___ my ma-ma made ___ for me.

4. So, with

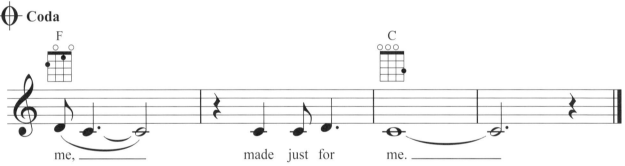

Coda

me, ___ made just for me. ___

Additional Lyrics

3. As she sewed, she told a story
From the Bible she had read,
About a coat of many colors
Joseph wore, and then she said,
"Perhaps this coat will bring you
Good luck and happiness."
And I just couldn't wait to wear it,
And Mama blessed it with a kiss.

4. So, with patches on my britches
And holes in both my shoes,
In my coat of many colors
I hurried off to school,
Just to find the others laughin'
And makin' fun of me
In my coat of many colors
My mama made for me.

5. And, oh, I couldn't understand it,
For I felt I was rich,
And I told 'em of the love
My mama sewed in ev'ry stitch.
And I told them all the story
Mama told me while she sewed,
And how my coat of many colors
Was worth more than all their clothes.

Counting Stars

Words and Music by Ryan Tedder

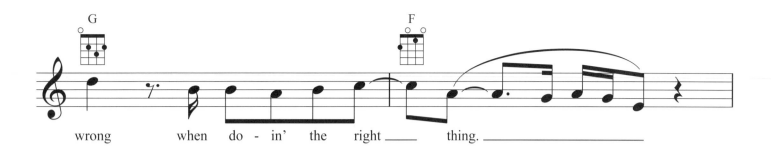

wrong   when   do - in'   the   right ____ thing. _____

I   could - n't lie,   could - n't   lie,   could - n't lie. ____

Ev - 'ry - thing _ that
Ev - 'ry - thing _ that

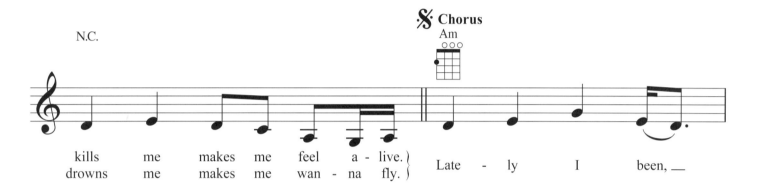

𝄋 Chorus

kills   me   makes   me   feel   a - live.
drowns   me   makes   me   wan - na   fly.

Late - ly   I   been, ____

I   been   los - in'   sleep ____   dream - in'   a - bout ____ the   things   that

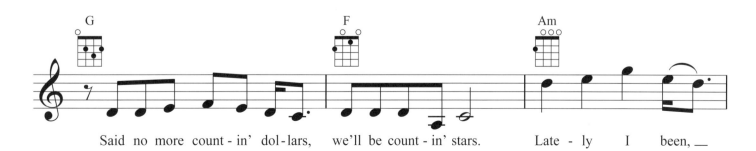

we   could   be.   But,   ba - by,   I   been, _   I   been   pray - in'   hard. ____

Said   no   more   count - in'   dol - lars,   we'll   be   count - in'   stars.   Late - ly   I   been, _

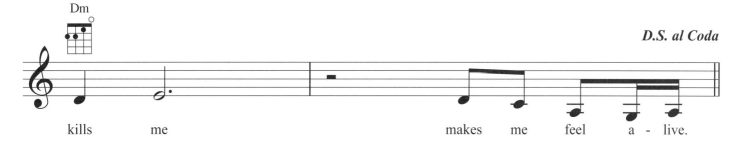

kills me   makes me feel a - live.

Coda
Outro-Bridge

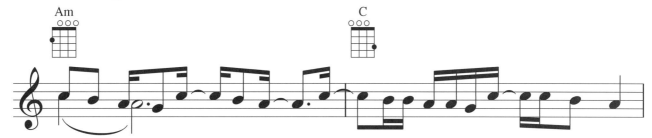

Take that mon- ey, watch _ it burn. _ Sink ___ in the riv - er the les - sons I've learned.
stars. _____

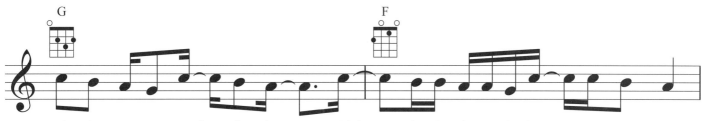

Take that mon- ey, watch _ it burn. _ Sink ___ in the riv - er the les - sons I've learned.

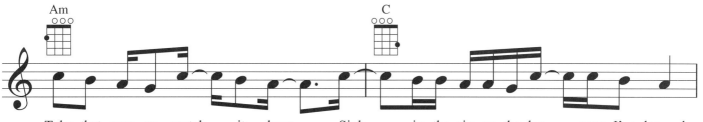

Take that mon- ey, watch _ it burn. _ Sink ___ in the riv - er the les - sons I've learned.

Take that mon- ey, watch _ it burn. _ Sink ___ in the riv - er the les - sons I've learned.

Additional Lyrics

2. I feel your love, and I feel it burn
 Down this river, every turn.
 Hope is a four-letter word.
 Make that money, watch it burn.

Drift Away

Words and Music by Mentor Williams

Oh, give me the beat, boys, and free my soul. I

wan - na get lost in your rock and roll and drift a - way.

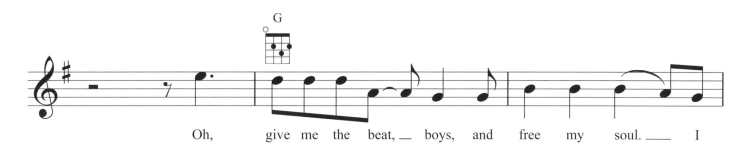

Oh, give me the beat, boys, and free my soul. I

wan - na get lost in your rock and roll and drift a - way.

To Coda ⊕

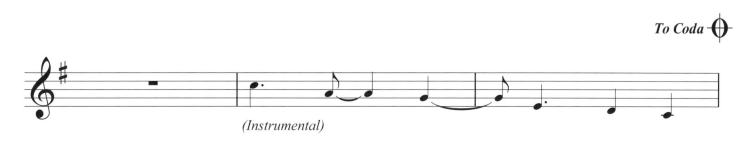

(Instrumental)

Additional Lyrics

2. Beginnin' to think that I'm wastin' time.
   I don't understand the things I do.
   The world outside looks so unkind,
   And I'm countin' on you to carry me through.

3. Thanks for the joy that you've given me.
   I want you to know I believe in your song
   And rhythm and rhyme and harmony.
   You help me along, makin' me strong.

Cups
(When I'm Gone)

from the Motion Picture Soundtrack PITCH PERFECT
Words and Music by A.P. Carter, Luisa Gerstein and Heloise Tunstall-Behrens

miss me by my hair, ___ you'll miss me ev - 'ry - where. _ Oh,
miss me by my walk, ___ you're gon - na miss me by my talk. _ Oh,

you're gon - na miss ___ me when I'm gone. When I'm
you're gon - na miss ___ me when I'm gone. When I'm

gone, when I'm gone, _____ you're gon - na miss ___ me when I'm
gone, when I'm gone, _____ you're gon - na miss ___ me when I'm

gone. You're gon - na miss me by my walk, ___ you're gon - na
gone. You're gon - na miss me by my hair, ___ you're gon - na

miss me by my talk. ___ Oh, ___ you're gon - na miss ___ me when I'm
miss me ev - 'ry - where. _ Oh, ___ you're sure gon - na miss me when I'm

gone.   2. I got my tick - et for the long way ___ 'round,

30

the one with the pret - ti - est ___ of views. It's got

moun - tains, it's got riv - ers, it's got sights to give you shiv - ers, ___ but it

D.S. al Coda

sure would be pret - ti - er ___ with you. When I'm

Coda

gone. When I'm

Outro-Chorus

gone, when I'm gone, ___ you're gon - na miss ___ me when I'm

gone. You're gon - na miss me by my walk, ___ you're gon - na

miss me by my talk. ___ Oh, you're gon - na miss ___ me when I'm gone.

Early Mornin' Rain

Words and Music by Gordon Lightfoot

First note

Verse
Brightly, in 2

1. In the ear - ly morn - in' rain _____
2.–4. *See additional lyrics*

with a dol - lar in ___ my hand, _____

with an ach - in' in my heart _____

and my pock - ets full of sand, _____

I'm a long way from home, _____

and I miss my loved ones so. _____

In the ear - ly morn - in' rain, _____

with no place to go. _____

1.–3.   4.

Additional Lyrics

2. Out on runway number nine,
   Big 707 set to go.
   But I'm stuck here in the grass
   Where the cold wind blows.
   Now the liquor tasted good,
   And the women all were fast.
   Well, there she goes, my friend,
   She's rollin' now at last.

3. Hear the mighty engines roar,
   See the silver bird on high.
   She's away and westward bound,
   Far above the clouds she'll fly,
   Where the mornin' rain don't fall
   And the sun always shines.
   She'll be flyin' o'er my home
   In about three hours' time.

4. This old airport's got me down;
   It's no earthly good to me.
   'Cause I'm stuck here on the ground,
   As cold and drunk as I can be.
   You can't jump a jet plane
   Like you can a freight train,
   So I'd best be on my way
   In the early mornin' rain.

Follow You Down

Words and Music by Bill Leen, Phil Rhodes, Jesse Valenzuela, Robin Wilson and D. Scott Johnson

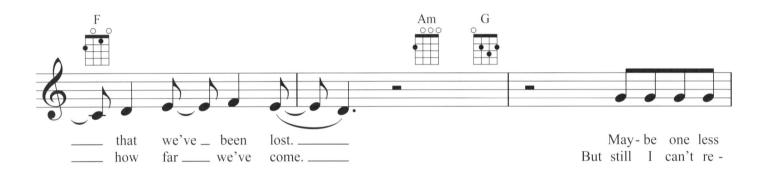

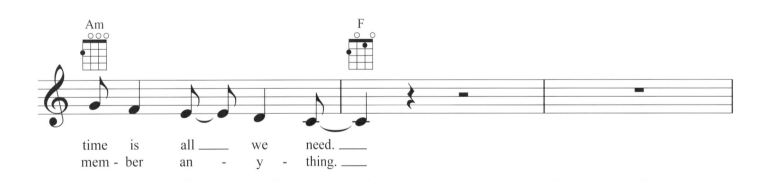

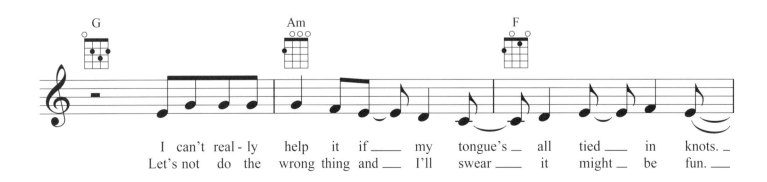

Jump - ing off a bridge, it's just ___ the far -
It's a long way down when all ___ the knots ___

Chorus

- thest that ___ I've ev - er been. ___
___ we've tied ___ have come ___ un - done. ___

An - y - where you go, ___

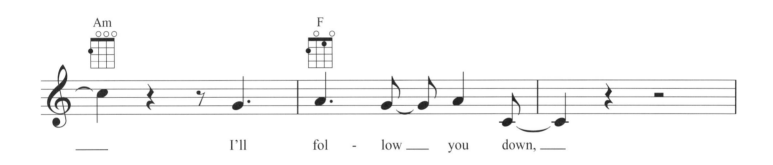

___ I'll fol - low ___ you down, ___

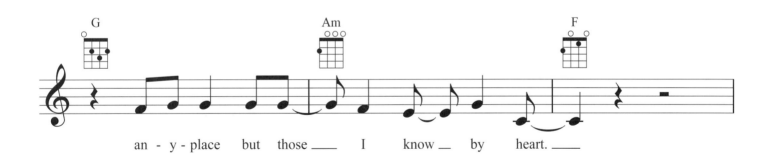

an - y - place but those ___ I know ___ by heart. ___

An - y - where you go, ___ I'll

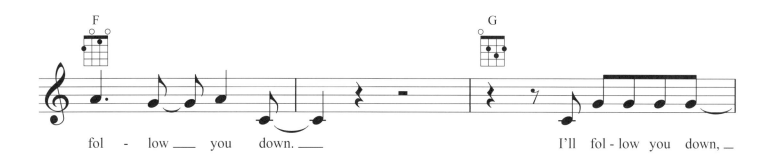

fol - low ___ you down. ___ I'll fol - low you down, ___

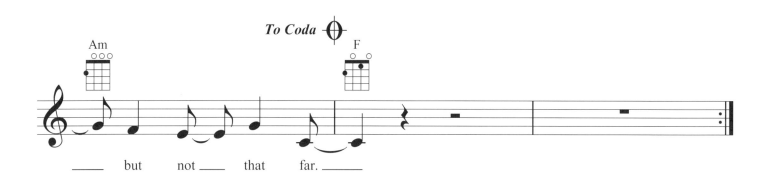

___ but not ___ that far. ___

Bridge

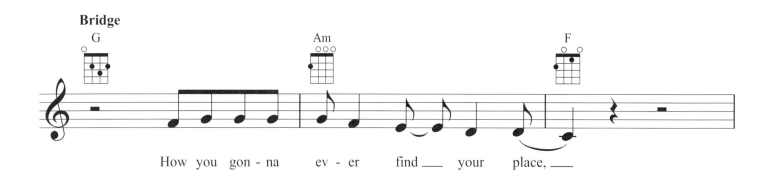

How you gon - na ev - er find ___ your place, ___

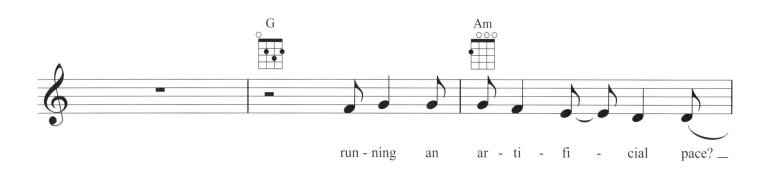

run - ning an ar - ti - fi - cial pace? ___

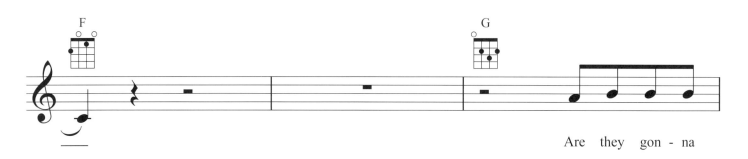

___ Are they gon - na

find us ly - ing face - down in ____ the sand? ____

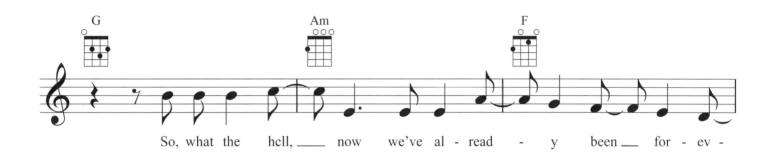

So, what the hell, ____ now we've al - read - y been ____ for - ev -

D.S. al Coda

Coda

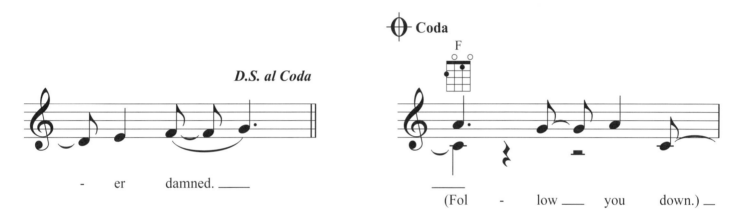

- er damned. ____

(Fol - low ____ you down.) ____

Outro

____

I'll fol - low you down, ____ but not ____ that far. ____

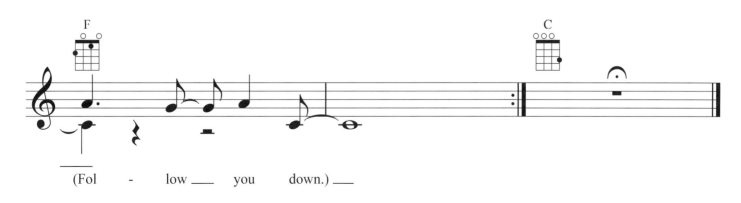

(Fol - low ____ you down.) ____

Girls Just Want to Have Fun

Words and Music by Robert Hazard

Verse
Bright Pop

1. I come home in the morn-ing light.__ My moth-
2., 3. *See additional lyrics*

-er says, "When __ you gon-na live your life right?" _

Oh, Ma-ma dear, __ we're not the for-tu- nate ones. And

girls, they wan-na have fu –un. Oh, __

1.

girls __ just wan- na have fun. __

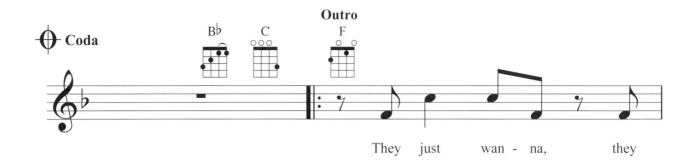

Coda

Outro

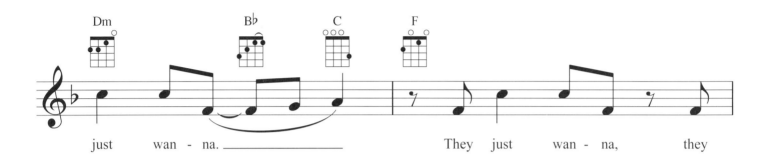

They just wan - na, they

just wan - na. _____ They just wan - na, they

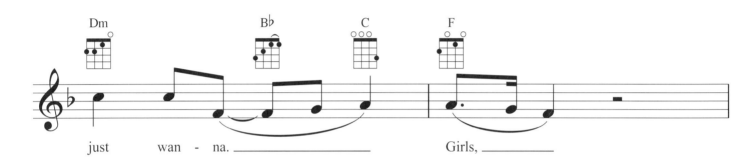

just wan - na. _____ Girls, _____

Repeat and fade

girls just wan - na have fun. _____

Additional Lyrics

2. The phone rings in the middle of the night.
   My father yells, "What you gonna do with your life?"
   Oh, Daddy dear, you know you're still number one.
   But girls, they wanna have fun.
   Oh, girls just wanna have... *(To Bridge)*

3. Some boys take a beautiful girl
   And hide her away from the rest of the world.
   I wanna be the one to walk in the sun.
   Oh, girls, they wanna have fun.
   Oh, girls just wanna have... *(To Bridge)*

Island in the Sun

Words and Music by Rivers Cuomo

First note

Verse
Moderately

1. When you're on _____ a hol - i - day, _____
2. When you're on _____ a gold - en sea, _____

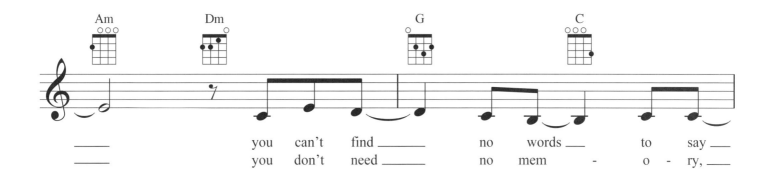

_____ you can't find _____ no words _____ to say _____
_____ you don't need _____ no mem - o - ry, _____

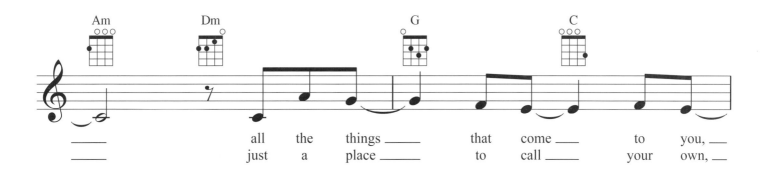

_____ all the things _____ that come _____ to you, _____
_____ just a place _____ to call _____ your own, _____

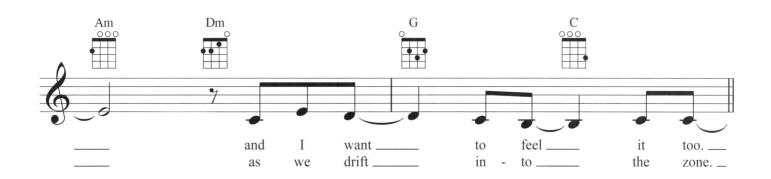

_____ and I want _____ to feel _____ it too. _____
_____ as we drift _____ in - to _____ the zone. _____

On an is - land in ____ the sun, ____

____ we'll be play - ing and hav - ing fun. ____

____ And it makes ____ me feel ____ so fine ____

____ I can't ____ con - trol ____ my brain. ____

Interlude

2., 3.

____ my brain. ____

Bridge

We'll run a -

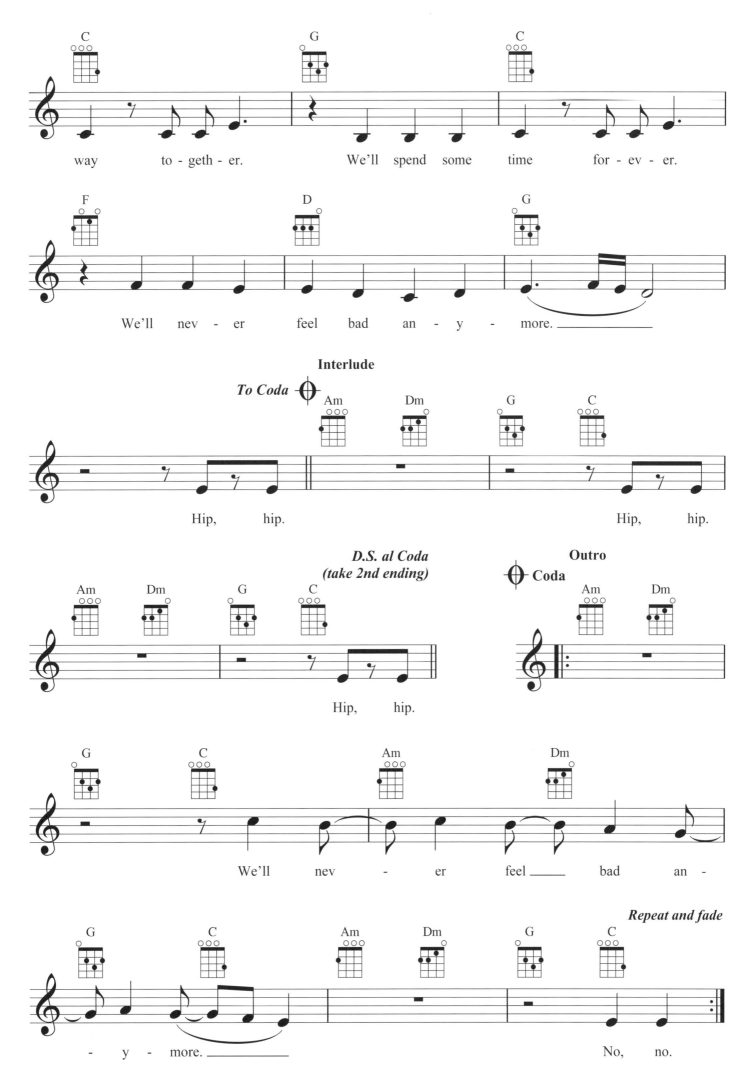

Good Riddance
(Time of Your Life)

Words by Billie Joe
Music by Green Day

Heartaches by the Number

Words and Music by Harlan Howard

Hickory Wind

Words and Music by Gram Parsons and Bob Buchanan

I   al - ways   pre - tend
each   time   it   be - gins
each   time   it   be - gins

that   I'm   get - ting   the   feel
call - ing   me   home,
call - ing   me   home,

of   hick - o - ry   wind.
hick - o - ry   wind.
hick - o - ry   wind.

1., 2.   3.

2. I   start - ed   out   Keeps
3. It's a   hard   way   to

Outro

call - ing   me   home, _____

hick - o - ry   wind.

I Have a Dream

Words and Music by Benny Andersson and Björn Ulvaeus

Chorus
F
C7
fail.
mile.
I be - lieve in an - gels,
B♭
F
some - thing good in ev - 'ry - thing I see. I be - lieve in
C7
B♭
an - gels when I know the time is right for
F
C7
me. I'll cross the stream, I have a
F
1.
2.
dream. 2. I have a I'll cross the
C7
F
stream, I have a dream.

I Knew You Were Trouble

Words and Music by Taylor Swift, Shellback and Max Martin

out _____ me, with - out _____ me, ee, ee, ee, ee. _____
now _____ I see, now _____ I see, ee, ee, ee, ee. _____

Pre-Chorus

And he's long _____ gone when he's next __
He was long _____ gone when he met __

_____ to __ me, and I re - a - lize _____
_____ me, and I re - a - lize _____

𝄋 **Chorus**

8va 2nd time

_____ the blame is on __ me. __ 'Cause } I knew you were
_____ the joke is on __ me. __

trou - ble when you walked in, _____ so shame on me now. __

__ Flew me to plac - es I'd nev - er been _____ till you

53

I'm So Lonesome I Could Cry

Words and Music by Hank Williams

First note

Verse
Plaintively

1. Hear _____ that lone - some whip - poor -
(3.) ev - er see _____ a rob - in

will? He sounds _____ too blue _____ to fly. _____
weep when sounds leaves _____ be - gan _____ to die? _____

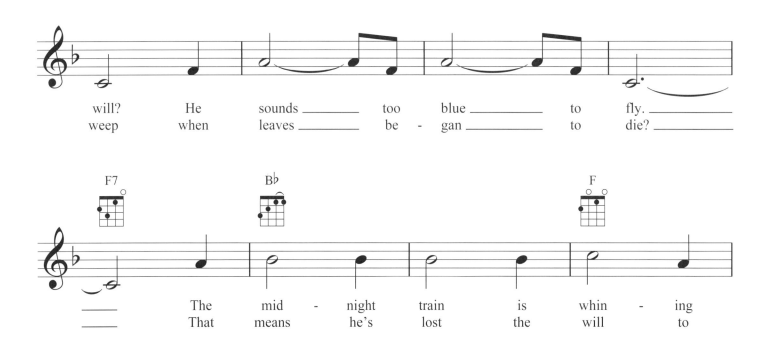

_____ The mid - night train is whin - ing
_____ That means he's lost the will to

low. I'm so lone - some I could _ cry. _____
live. I'm so lone - some I could _ cry. _____

Verse

_____ 2. I've nev - er seen _____ a night _____ so
_____ 4. The si - lence of _____ a fall - ing

long when time _____ goes crawl - ing by. _____ The
star when lights up _____ a pur - ple sky. _____ And

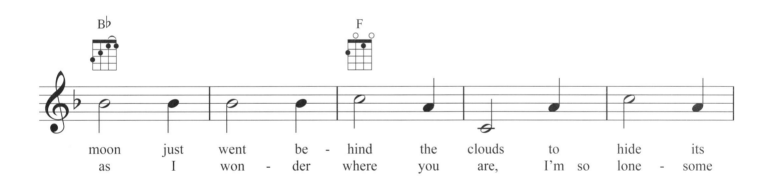

moon just went be - hind the clouds to hide its
as I won - der where you are, I'm so lone - some

face and __ cry. _____ 3. Did you
I could _ cry. _____

Jolene

Words and Music by Dolly Parton

Jo - lene, Jo - lene, Jo - lene, Jo - lene, _____ I'm

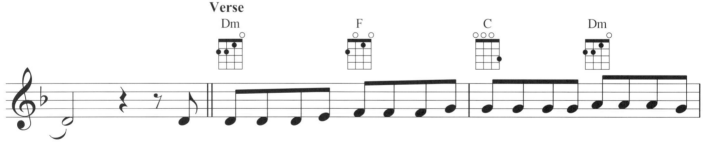

beg-ging of you, please don't take my man. __ Jo - lene, Jo-lene, Jo -

lene, Jo - lene, _____ please don't take him just be - cause you can. _____

Verse

Dm   F   C   Dm

___ 1. Your beau - ty is be - yond com - pare, with flam - ing locks of au-burn hair, with
    3. You could have your choice of men, but I could nev - er love a - gain. __

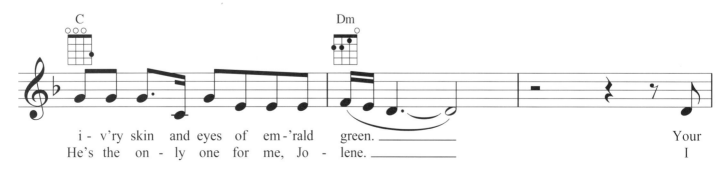

i - v'ry skin and eyes of em-'rald green. _____ Your
He's the on - ly one for me, Jo - lene. _____ I

smile is like a breath of spring, your voice is soft like sum-mer rain, and
had to have this talk with you, my hap-pi-ness de-pends on you and

I can-not com-pete with you, __ Jo - lene.   2. He
what-ev-er you de-cide to do, __ Jo - lene.   Jo -

Verse

talks a-bout you in his sleep and there's noth-ing I can do to keep from

cry-in' when he calls your name, Jo - lene. _____   And

I can eas-'ly un-der-stand how you could eas-'ly take my man, but you

don't know what he means to me, Jo - lene.   Jo -

It's Hard to Be Humble

Words and Music by Mac Davis

First note

Oh, Lord, it's hard ___ to be hum - ble

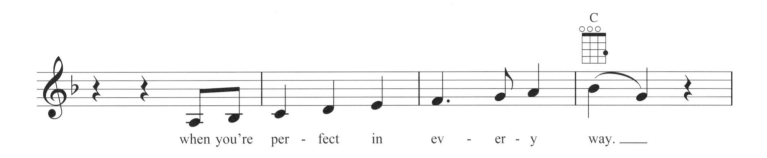

when you're per - fect in ev - er - y way. ___

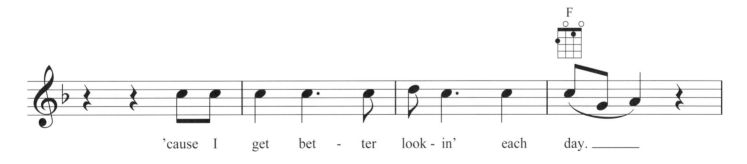

I can't wait to look in ___ the mir - ror

'cause I get bet - ter look - in' each day. ___

To know me is to love me, I

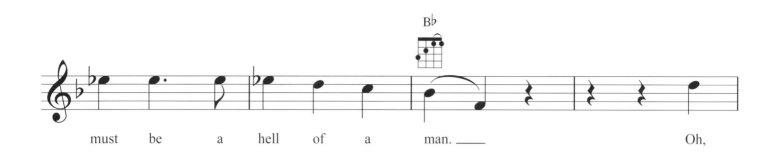

must be a hell of a man. _____ Oh,

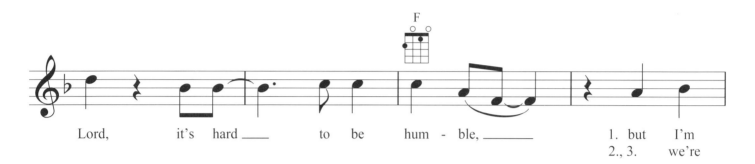

Lord, it's hard _____ to be hum - ble, _____ 1. but I'm
2., 3. we're

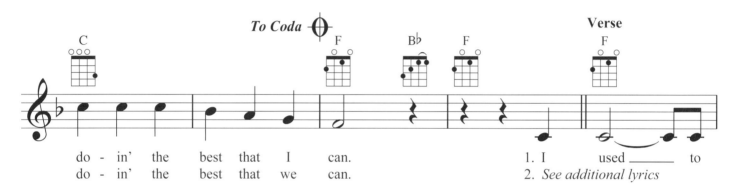

To Coda ⊕ **Verse**

do - in' the best that I can. 1. I used _____ to
do - in' the best that we can. 2. *See additional lyrics*

have a girl - friend, but I guess she just could-n't com -

pete with all _____ of these love - starved _

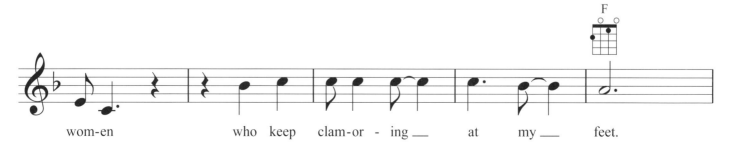

wom-en who keep clam-or - ing _____ at my _____ feet.

Additional Lyrics

2. I guess you could say I'm a loner, a cowboy outlaw, tough and proud.
   Oh, I could have lots of friends if I wanna, but then I wouldn't stand out from the crowd.
   Some folks say that I'm egotistical. Hell, I don't even know what that means.
   I guess it has something to do with the way that I fill out my skin-tight blue jeans.

Last Kiss

Words and Music by Wayne Cochran

First note

Intro-Chorus
Moderately fast

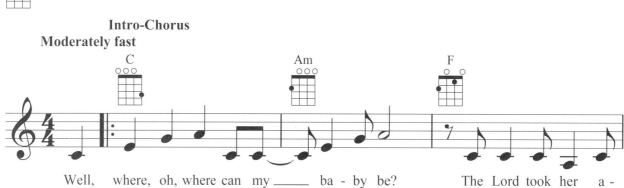

Well, where, oh, where can my _____ ba-by be? The Lord took her a-

way from me. _____ She's gone to heav-en, so I got to be good _____ so

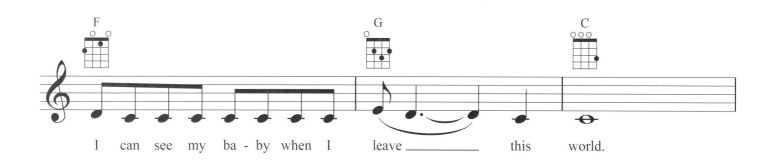

I can see my ba-by when I leave _____ this world.

Verse

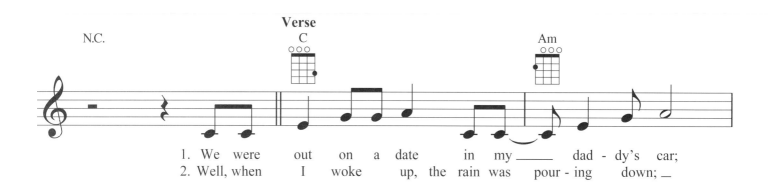

1. We were out on a date in my _____ dad-dy's car;
2. Well, when I woke up, the rain was pour-ing down; _____

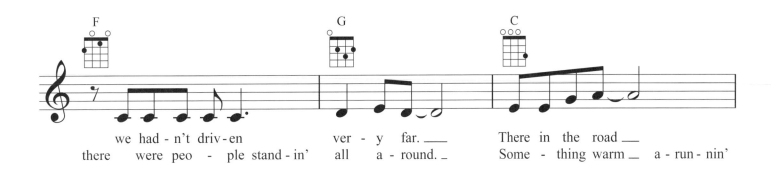

we had - n't driv - en / ver - y far. __ / There in the road __
there were peo - ple stand - in' / all a - round. _ / Some - thing warm __ a - run - nin'

straight a - head, __ / a car was stalled; the / en - gine was dead. __
in my eyes, __ / but I found __ my ba - by / some - how that night. __ I

I could - n't stop, __ / so I swerved to the right. __ / I'll nev - er for - get __ the
raised her head __ and then she smiled and said, __ / "Hold me, dar - ling, for a

sound that night: __ / the cry - in' tires, __ / the bust - in' glass, __ the
lit - tle while." _ I / held her close, __ I kissed her / our last kiss. __ I

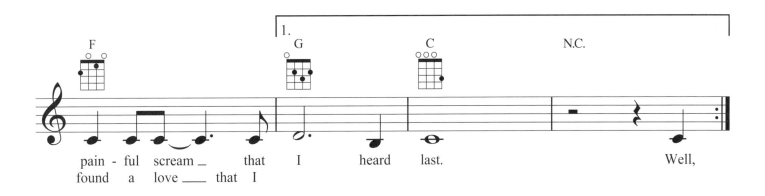

1.

pain - ful scream __ that I / heard last. / Well,
found a love __ that I

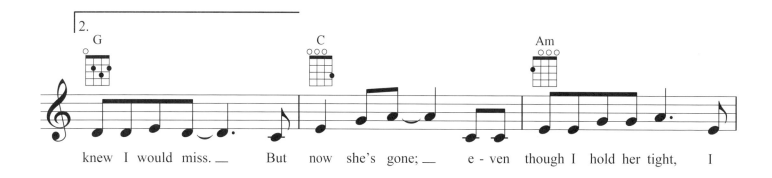

knew I would miss. __ But now she's gone; __ e - ven though I hold her tight, I

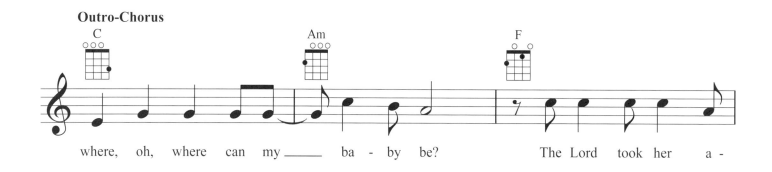

lost my love, __ my life that night. Well,

Outro-Chorus

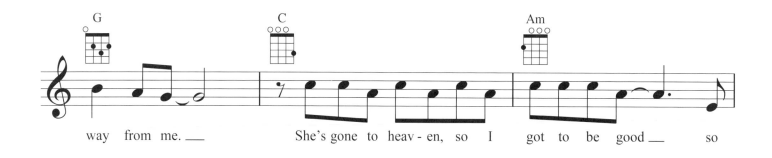

where, oh, where can my ____ ba - by be? The Lord took her a -

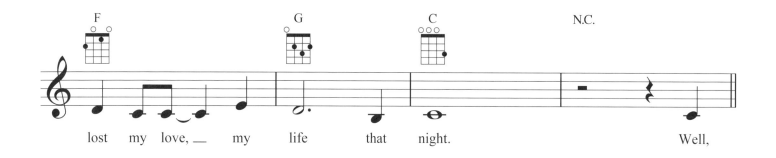

way from me. __ She's gone to heav - en, so I got to be good __ so

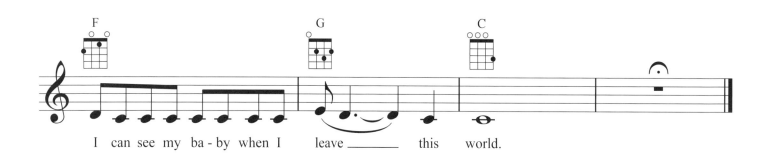

I can see my ba - by when I leave ____ this world.

One of Us

Words and Music by Eric Bazilian

First note

Verse
Moderately

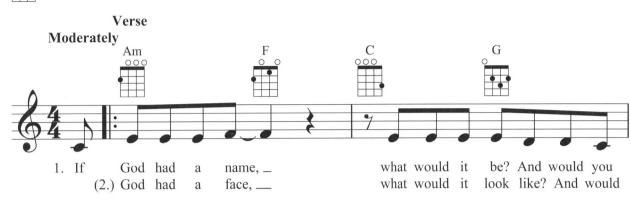

1. If God had a name, ___ what would it be? And would you
(2.) God had a face, ___ what would it look like? And would

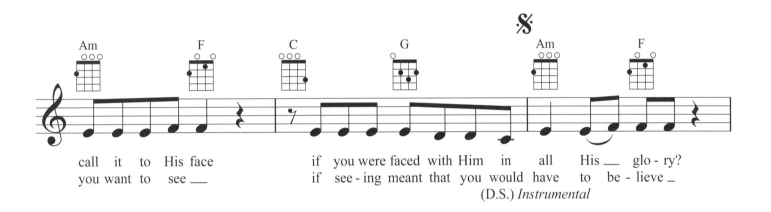

call it to His face if you were faced with Him in all His ___ glo - ry?
you want to see ___ if see - ing meant that you would have to be - lieve ___
(D.S.) *Instrumental*

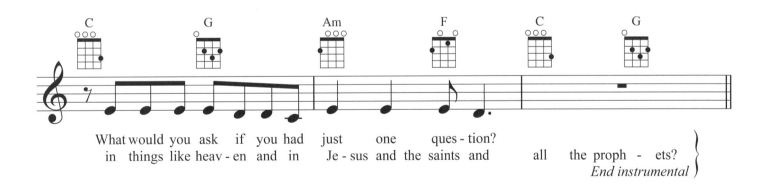

What would you ask if you had just one ques - tion?
in things like heav - en and in Je - sus and the saints and all the proph - ets?
End instrumental

Pre-Chorus

Yeah, yeah, God is ___ great. Yeah, yeah, God is ___ good.

Yeah, yeah, yeah, yeah, yeah. What if God was one of us,

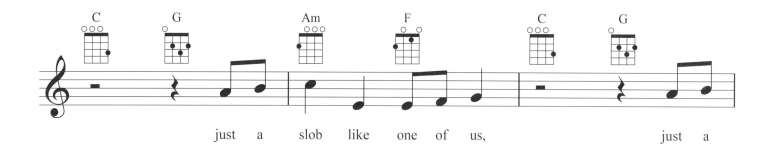

just a slob like one of us, just a

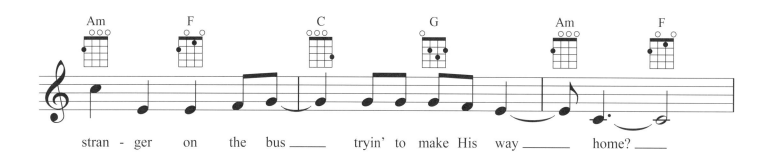

stran-ger on the bus _____ tryin' to make His way _____ home? _____

2. If Tryin' to make His way _____ home, _____

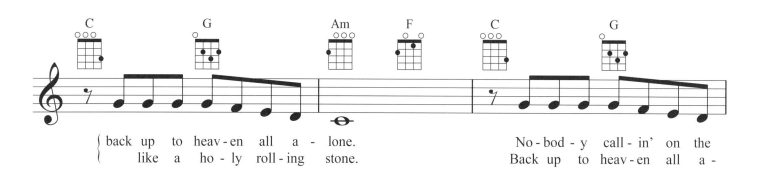

{ back up to heav-en all a-lone.
{ like a ho-ly roll-ing stone.

No-bod-y call-in' on the
Back up to heav-en all a-

phone,
lone,
'cept for the Pope may - be in _____ Rome. _____

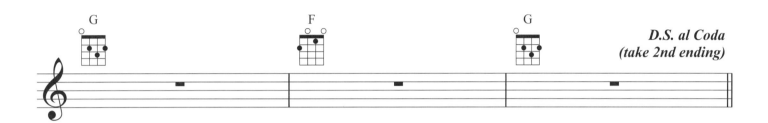

just tryin' to make His way _____ home. _____

No - bod - y call - in' on the phone,

'cept for the Pope may - be in Rome.

The Last Thing on My Mind

Words and Music by Tom Paxton

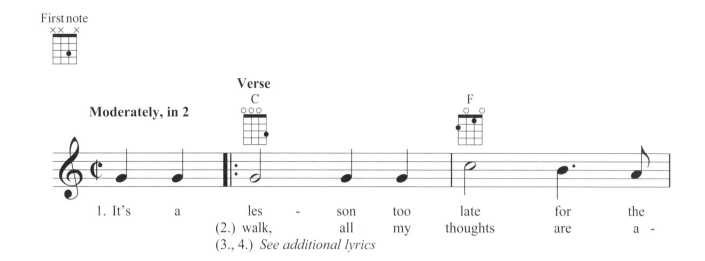

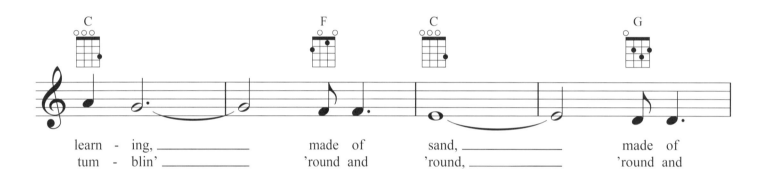

1. It's a les - son too late for the
(2.) walk, all my thoughts are a -
(3., 4.) *See additional lyrics*

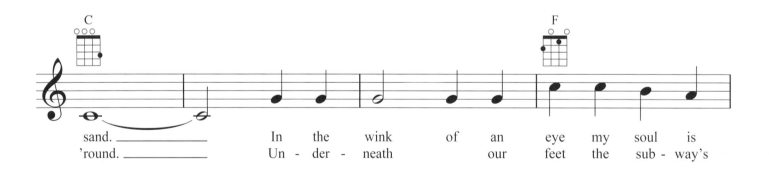

learn - ing, _____ made of sand, _____ made of
tum - blin' _____ 'round and 'round, _____ 'round and

sand. _____ In the wink of an eye my soul is
'round. _____ Un - der - neath our feet the sub - way's

turn - ing _____ in your hand, _____ in your
rum - blin' _____ un - der - ground, _____ un - der -

Chorus

hand. _____
ground. _____

Are you go - ing a - way with no word of fare - well? Will there be not a trace left be - hind? _____ Well, I could have loved you bet - ter, did - n't mean to be un - kind. You know that was the last thing on my

1.–3.
mind. _____ 2. As we mind. _____

Additional Lyrics

3. You've got reasons a-plenty for goin'
   This I know, this I know.
   For the weeds have been steadily growing.
   Please don't go, please don't go.

4. As I lie in my bed in the morning
   Without you, without you,
   Each song in my breast dies a-borning,
   Without you, without you.

Move It On Over

Words and Music by Hank Williams

Verse

changed the lock on our front door; ___ now my door key don't
told me not to play a - round, ___ but I done let the

fit no more. ___ So, get it on o - ver.
deal go down. ___ So, pack it on o - ver.

(Move it on o - ver.) Scoot it on o - ver.
(Move it on o - ver.) Tote it on o - ver.

(Move it on o - ver.) Move o - ver, skin - ny dog, 'cause the
(Move it on o - ver.) Move o - ver, nice ___ dog, 'cause a

fat dog's mov - in' _____ in.
bad dog's mov - in' _____

3. This   in. _____

100 Years

Words and Music by John Ondrasik

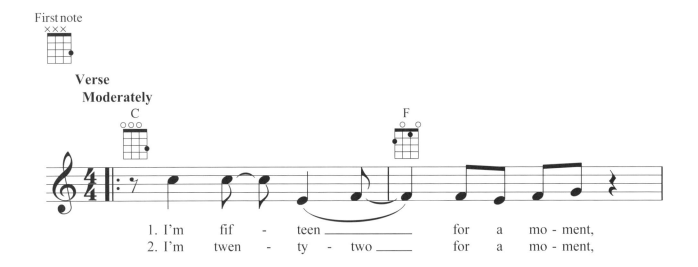

First note

Verse
Moderately

1. I'm fif - teen _____ for a mo - ment,
2. I'm twen - ty - two _____ for a mo - ment,

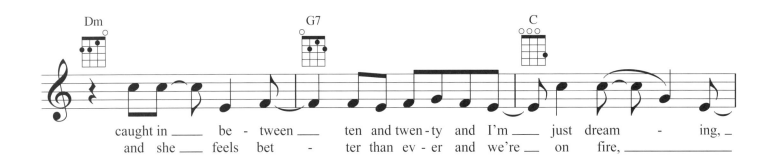

caught in _____ be - tween _____ ten and twen - ty and I'm _____ just dream - ing, _____
and she _____ feels bet - ter than ev - er and we're _____ on fire, _____

_____ count - ing the ways _____ to where you are. _____
mak - ing our way _____ back _____ from Mars. _____

Chorus

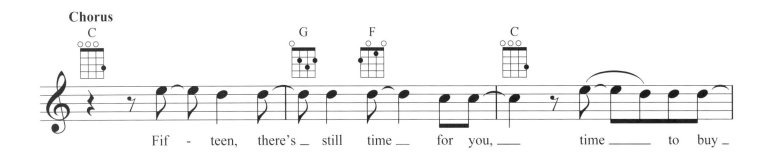

Fif - teen, there's _____ still time _____ for you, _____ time _____ to buy _____

and time to lose. Fif - teen, there's nev - er a wish

bet - ter than this when you on - ly got a hun -

- dred years to live.

Verse

3. I'm thir - ty - three

for a mo - ment, I'm still the man, but you see I'm a they;

a kid on the way, a fam - 'ly on my mind.

Verse

4. I'm for - ty - five ____ for a mo - ment,

the sea ____ is high ____ and I'm head - ing in - to ____ a cri - sis, ____

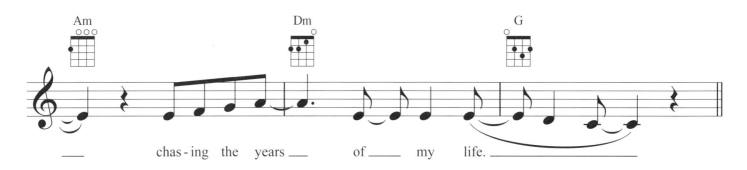

____ chas - ing the years ____ of ____ my life. ____

Chorus

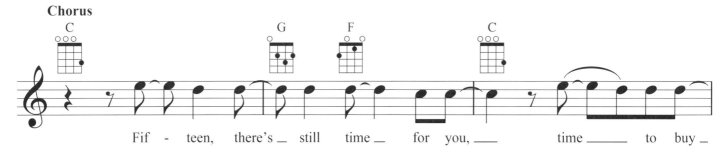

Fif - teen, there's __ still time __ for you, ____ time ____ to buy __

____ and time __ to lose ____ your - self ____ with - in ____ a morn - ing star. __

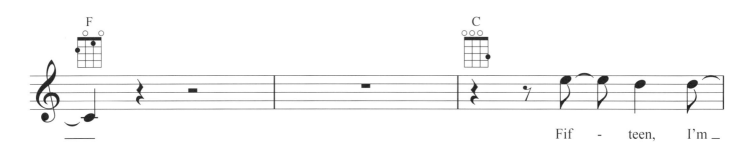

Fif - teen, I'm __

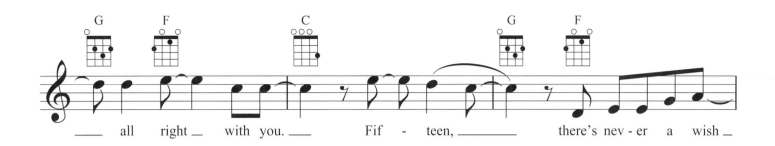

_____ all right _____ with you. _____ Fif - teen, _____ there's nev - er a wish _____

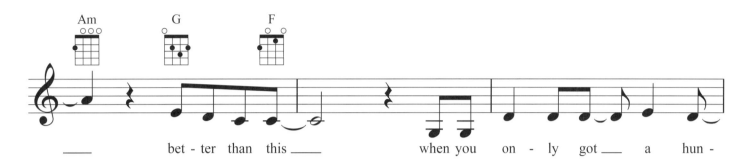

_____ bet - ter than this _____ when you on - ly got _____ a hun -

Bridge

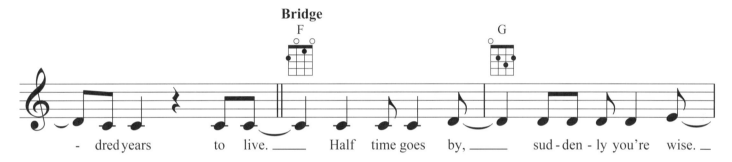

- dred years to live. _____ Half time goes by, _____ sud - den - ly you're wise. _____

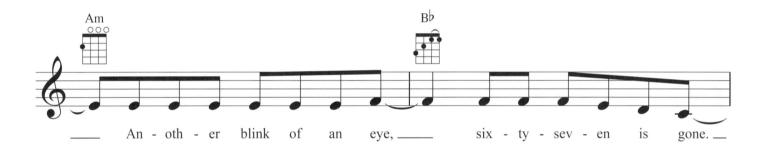

_____ An - oth - er blink of an eye, _____ six - ty - sev - en is gone. _____

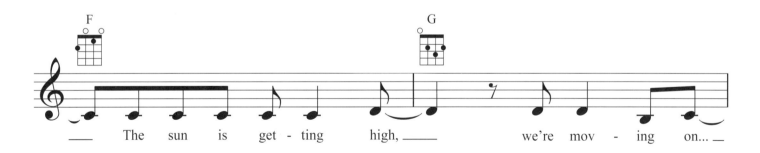

_____ The sun is get - ting high, _____ we're mov - ing on... _____

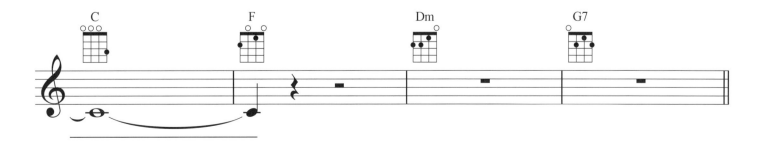

5. I'm nine - ty - nine ____ for a mo - ment, I'm dying __ for just __

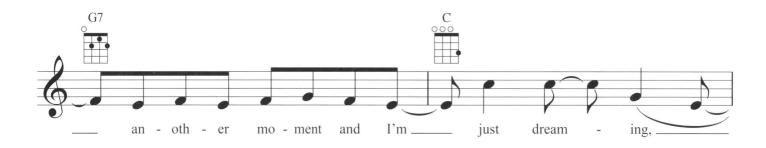

____ an - oth - er mo - ment and I'm ____ just dream - ing, ____

____ count - ing the ways ____ to where you are. ____

Chorus

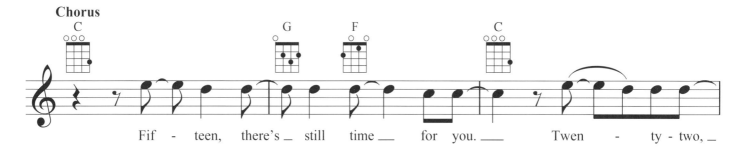

Fif - teen, there's __ still time __ for you. ____ Twen - ty - two, __

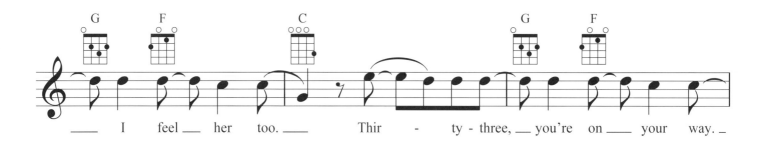

____ I feel __ her too. ____ Thir - ty - three, __ you're on ____ your way. __

Interlude

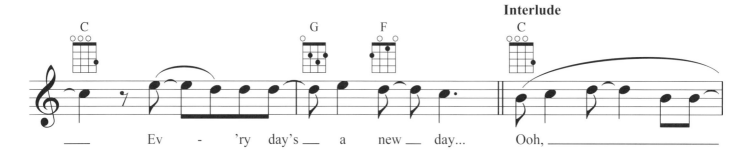

____ Ev - 'ry day's __ a new __ day... Ooh, ____

ooh,

ooh.

Outro-Chorus

Fif - teen, there's ___ still time ___ for you, ___ time ___ to buy ___ and time ___ to choose. ___ Hey, fif - teen, there's nev - er a wish ___ bet - ter than this ___ when you on - ly got ___ a hun - dred years to live. ___

Please Come to Boston

Words and Music by Dave Loggins

Verse
Moderately slow

1. Please come to Bos - ton for the spring - time. I'm
2. Please come to Den - ver with the snow - fall. We'll
3. Please come to L. ___ A. to live for - ev - er. A

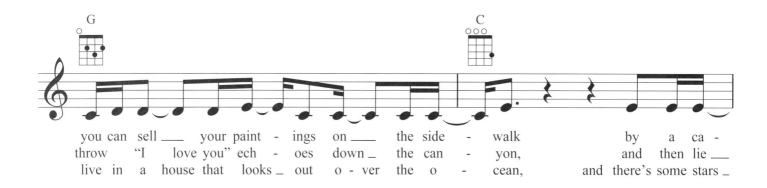

stay - ing here ___ with some friends ___ and they've ___ got lots ___ of room, ___ and
move up in - to the moun - tains ___ so far ___ that we can't be found, ___ and
Cal - i - for - nia life a - lone is just ___ too hard ___ to build. ___ I

you can sell ___ your paint - ings on ___ the side - walk by a ca -
throw "I love you" ech - oes down ___ the can - yon, and then lie ___
live in a house that looks ___ out o - ver the o - cean, and there's some stars ___

- fé where ___ I hope ___ to be ___ work - ing soon. ___
___ a - wake ___ at night ___ un - til they come back a - round. ___
___ that fell ___ from the sky and liv - ing up on the hill. ___

Please come to Bos - ton. She said, "No, _____ would you come home _ to me?" _
Please come to Den - ver. She said, "No, _____ would you come home _ to me?" _
Please come to L. _ A. She said, "No, _____ would you come home _ to me?" _

Chorus

_____ And she said, _ "Hey, ram - blin' boy, _ now won't you set - tle down?
_____ And she said, _ "Hey, ram - blin' boy, _ why don't you set - tle down?
_____ And she said, _ "Hey, ram - blin' boy, _ why don't you set - tle down?

Bos - ton ain't _ your kind of town. _ }
Den - ver ain't _ your kind of town. _ } There ain't no gold _ and there ain't _ no - bod - y like
L. A. can't be your kind of town. _ }

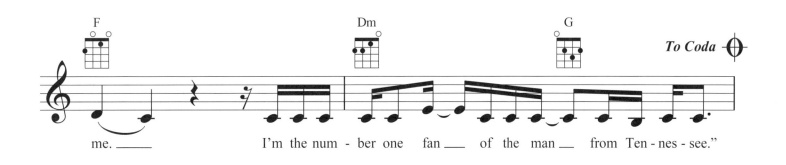

To Coda ⊕

me. _____ I'm the num - ber one fan _ of the man _ from Ten - nes - see."

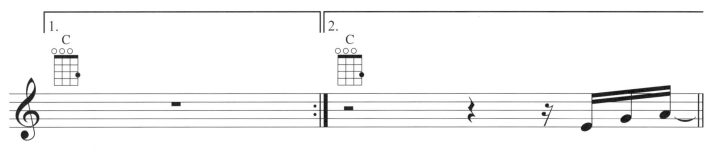

1.   2.

Now this drift -

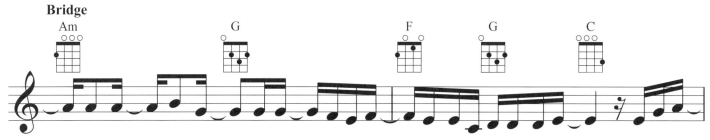

- er's world __ goes round __ and round __ and I doubt __ that it's ev-er gon-na stop. __ But of all __

__ the dreams __ I've lost __ or found __ and all _____ that I _____ ain't got, __ I still need to

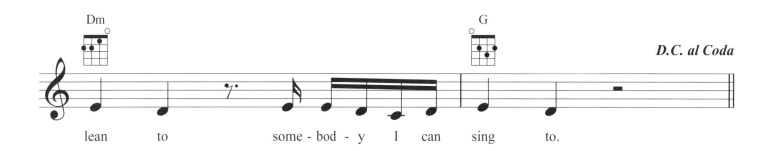

lean to some-bod-y I can sing to.

D.C. al Coda

Coda

Outro

I'm the num - ber one fan __ of the man __ from Ten-nes-see. __

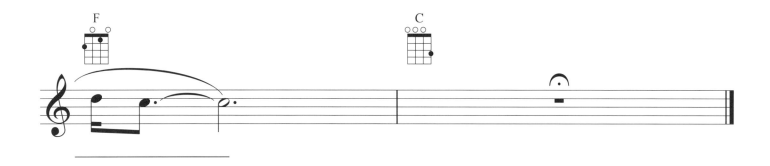

Paradise

Words and Music by Guy Berryman, Jon Buckland, Will Champion, Chris Martin and Brian Eno

Interlude

Verse

par - a - par - a - par - a - dise, par - a - par - a -

- par - a - dise, par - a - par - a - par - a - dise.

Bridge

Oh, _____ oh. _____ La, la, _____ la, la, la,

la, la, _____ la, la, la, la, la, _____ la, la, la, _____ la, la. And so ly -

- ing un - der - neath _____ those storm - y skies, _____

_____ she said, "Oh, _____ I know the

Perfect

Words and Music by Ed Sheeran

time. _____ Dar - ling, just kiss me slow, your heart is
time. _____ Dar - ling, just hold my hand. Be my girl, I'll

all ____ I ____ own. And in your eyes, you're ____ hold - ing mine. _
be ____ your ____ man. I've seen the fu - ture ____ in your eyes. _

Chorus

___ } Ba - by, _____ I'm danc - ing in the

dark with you be - tween my arms. Bare - foot on the

grass, lis - ten - ing to our ___ fa - v'rite song. { When you said you looked a
{ When I saw you in that

To Coda ⊕

mess, I whis-pered un - der-neath my breath. But you heard it, "Dar - ling,
dress, look - ing so beau - ti - ful, I don't ___ de - serve this. "Dar - ling,

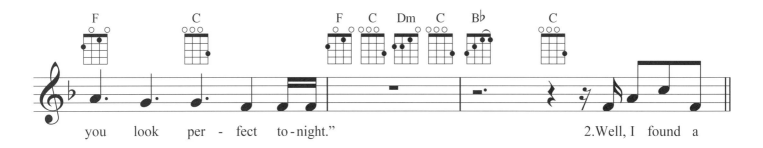

you look per - fect to-night." 2.Well, I found a

Verse

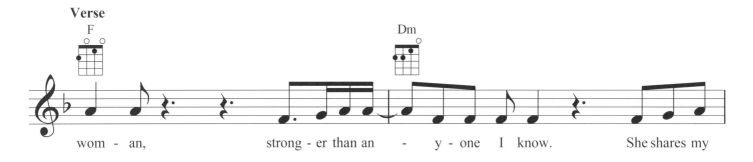

wom - an, strong - er than an - y - one I know. She shares my

dreams; I hope __ that some-day I'll share her home. _____ I found a love __

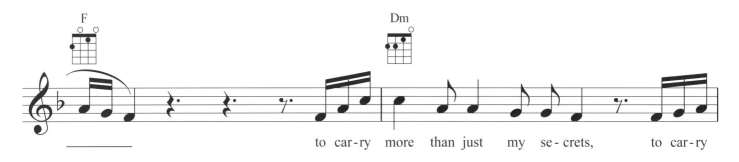

_____ to car-ry more than just my se - crets, to car-ry

love, to car-ry chil - dren of our own. _____ We are still kids, but we're

D.S. al Coda

Coda **Interlude**

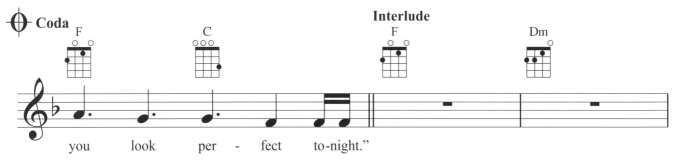

you look per - fect to-night."

Outro-Chorus

Ba - by, _____ I'm _____ danc - ing in the dark with you be - tween my arms. Bare - foot on the grass, lis - ten - ing to our ___ fa - v'rite song. I have faith in what _ I see. Now I know I have met an an - gel in per - son, and she looks per - fect. I don't de - serve this, you look per - fect to-night.

Right Here Waiting

Words and Music by Richard Marx

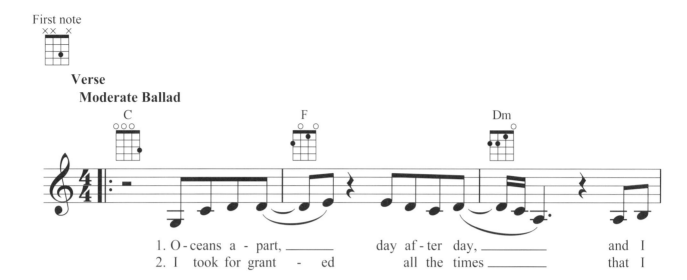

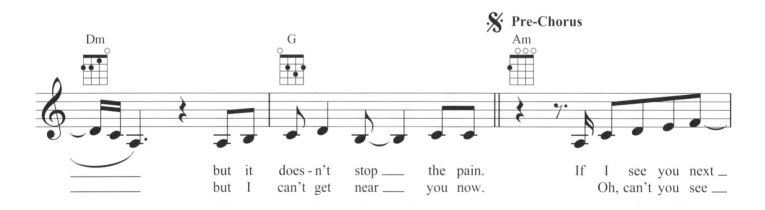

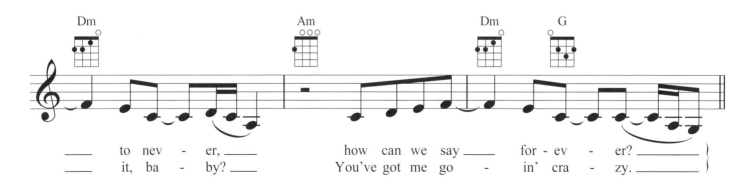

Chorus

Wher - ev - er you go, _____ what - ev - er you do, _____ I will ___ be right _____ here wait - ing for you. _____

What - ev - er it takes, _____ or how my heart breaks, _____

To Coda

1. I will ___ be right _____ here wait - ing for you. _____

2. **Bridge**

_____ I won - der how we can ___ sur - vive _____ this ro - mance. _____ But in the

end, if I'm ___ with you, ___ I'll take ___ the chance. ___

Interlude

D.S. al Coda
(Lyric 2)

Coda
Outro

Wait - ing for you. _____

Save Tonight

Words and Music by Eagle Eye Cherry

First note

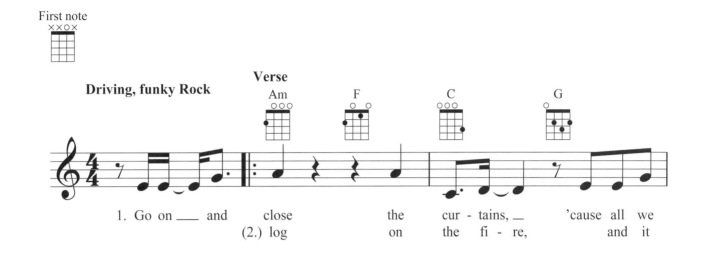

Driving, funky Rock

Verse

1. Go on ___ and close   the   cur - tains, ___   'cause all we
(2.) log   on   the   fi - re,   and it

need   is   can - dle - light.   You and ___ me,   and a
burns   like   me ___ for ___ you.   To - mor - row comes   with

bot - tle of wine, ___   gon - na hold   you to - night,   ah, yeah. ___   Well, we
one de - si - re,   to take   me a - way,   it's true. ___   It ain't

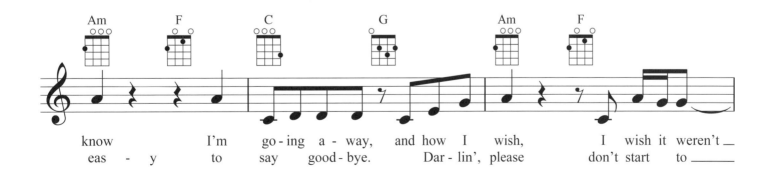

know   I'm   go - ing a - way,   and how I wish,   I wish it weren't ___
eas - y   to   say   good - bye.   Dar - lin', please   don't start to ___

Save the Last Dance for Me

Words and Music by Doc Pomus and Mort Shuman

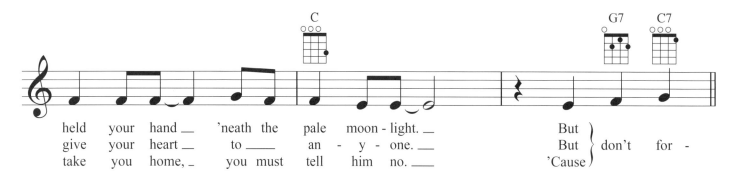

Chorus

get who's tak - ing you home and in whose arms you're gon - na be. ___

To Coda ⊕

So, dar - lin', ___ save the last dance for

1. me.

2. Oh, I me.

Ba - by, don't you know I

Bridge

love you so? ___ Can't you feel it when we touch?

I will nev - er nev - er let you go. ___ I love you, oh, so

D.S. al Coda

much. 3. You can

⊕ **Coda**

me. ___

Seven Bridges Road

Words and Music by Stephen T. Young

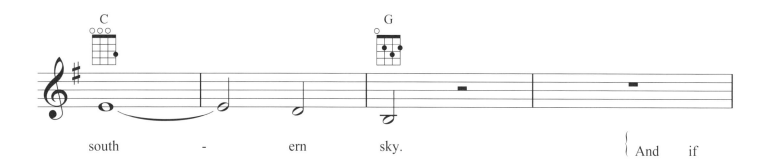

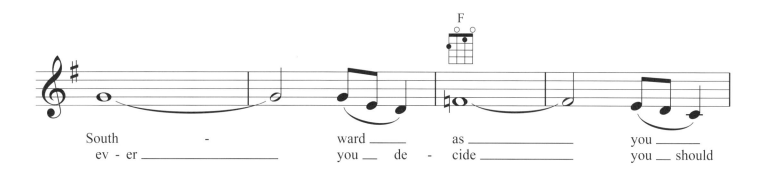

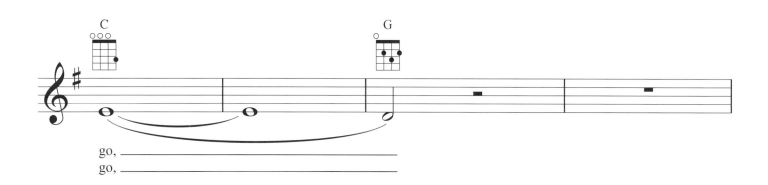

there _____ is _____ moon - light _ and
there _____ is _____ a taste _____ of _____

moss _____ in the trees
time - sweet - ened hon - ey } down the

Sev - en _____ Bridg - es _____

Bright Country, in 2

To Coda ⊕ G

Road. _____

Verse

G

2. Now, I _____ have _____
(3.) I _____ have _____

F   C

loved _____ you _____ like a ba -
loved _____ you _____ in a tame _

- by,
___ way,

like _____ some _____
and I _____ have _____

lone - some _____ child. _____
loved _____ you _____ wild. _____

1.

___
___

3. And

2.

Bridge

Some - times _____ there's _____

___ a part _____ of me _____

has to turn _____ from here _____

Shelter from the Storm

Words and Music by Bob Dylan

First note

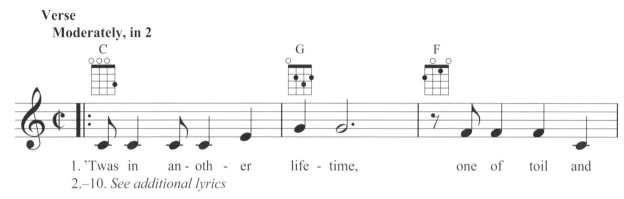

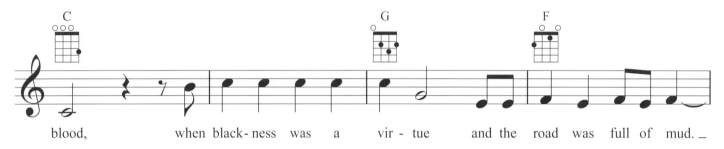

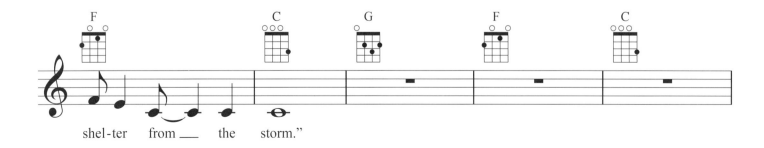

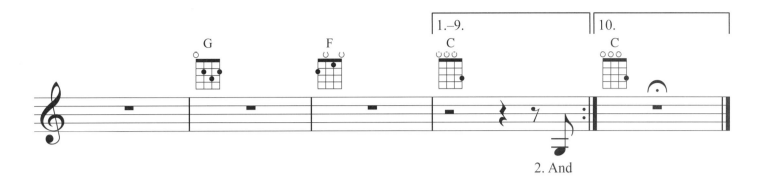

Additional Lyrics

2. And if I pass this way again, you can rest assured
   I'll always do my best for her; on that I give my word.
   In a world of steel-eyed death and men who are fighting to be warm,
   "Come in," she said, "I'll give ya shelter from the storm."

3. Not a word was spoke between us; there was little risk involved.
   Everything up to that point had been left unresolved.
   Try imagining a place where it's always safe and warm.
   "Come in," she said, "I'll give ya shelter from the storm."

4. I was burned out from exhaustion, buried in the hail,
   Poisoned in the bushes and blown out on the trail,
   Hunted like a crocodile, ravaged in the corn.
   "Come in," she said, "I'll give ya shelter from the storm."

5. Suddenly, I turned around and she was standin' there
   With silver bracelets on her wrists and flowers in her hair.
   She walked up to me so gracefully and took my crown of thorns.
   "Come in," she said, "I'll give ya shelter from the storm."

6. Now there's a wall between us; somethin' there's been lost.
   I took too much for granted; I got my signals crossed.
   Just to think that it all began on a non-eventful morn.
   "Come in," she said, "I'll give ya shelter from the storm."

7. Well, the deputy walks on hard nails and the preacher rides a mount,
   But nothing really matters much; it's doom alone that counts.
   And the one-eyed undertaker, he blows a futile horn.
   "Come in," she said, "I'll give ya shelter from the storm."

8. I've heard newborn babies wailin' like a mournin' dove
   And old men with broken teeth stranded without love.
   Do I understand your question, man? Is it hopeless and forlorn?
   "Come in," she said, "I'll give ya shelter from the storm."

9. In a little hilltop village, they gambled for my clothes.
   I bargained for salvation and she gave me a lethal dose.
   I offered up my innocence; I got repaid with scorn.
   "Come in," she said, "I'll give ya shelter from the storm."

10. Well, I'm livin' in a foreign country, but I'm bound to cross the line.
    Beauty walks a razor's edge; someday I'll make it mine.
    If I could only turn back the clock to when God and her were born.
    "Come in," she said, "I'll give ya shelter from the storm."

Slip Slidin' Away

Words and Music by Paul Simon

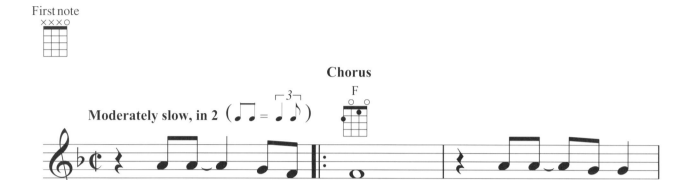

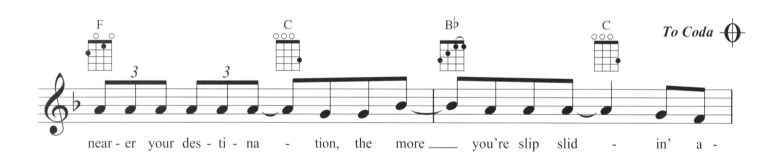

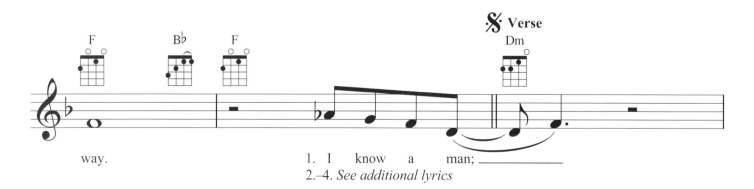

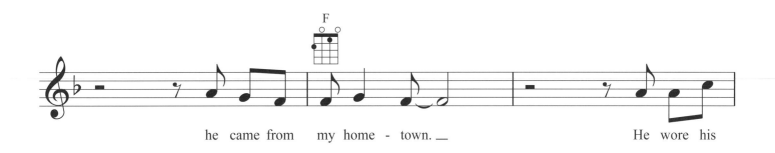

he came from my home - town. ___ He wore his

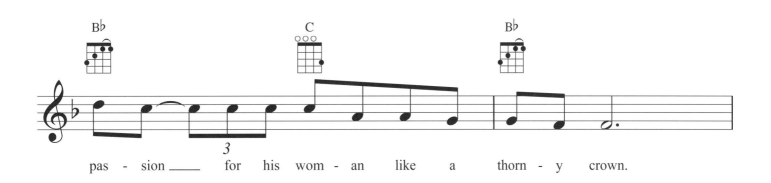

pas - sion ___ for his wom - an like a thorn - y crown.

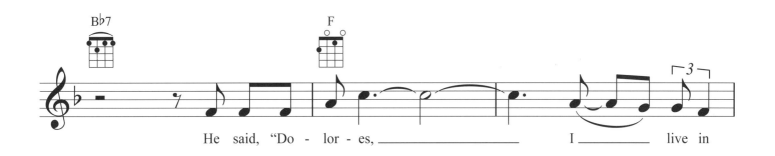

He said, "Do - lor - es, ___ I ___ live in

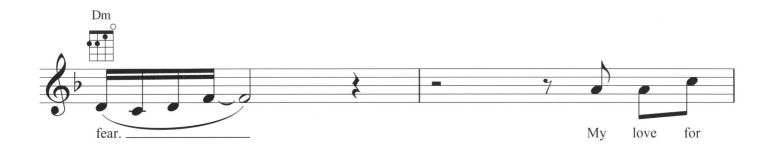

fear. ___ My love for

you's so o - ver - pow'r - ing I'm a - fraid ___ that I ___ will dis - ap -

pear." Slip slid - in' a - way. _____

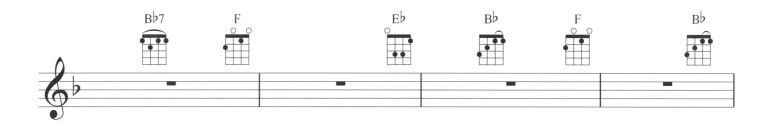

D.S. al Coda
(with repeat)

4. God on - ly knows. _

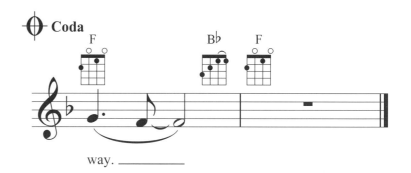

⊕ **Coda**

way. _____

Additional Lyrics

2. And I know a woman; became a wife.
   These are the very words she uses to describe her life.
   She said, "A good day ain't got no rain."
   She said, "A bad day's when I lie in bed and think of things that might have been."

3. And I know a father who had a son.
   He longed to tell him all the reasons for the things he'd done.
   He came a long way just to explain.
   He kissed his boy as he lay sleeping, then he turned around and headed home again.

4. God only knows. God makes His plan.
   The information's unavailable to the mortal man.
   We're workin' our jobs, collect our pay,
   Believe we're glidin' down the highway, when in fact, we're slip slidin' away.

The Scientist

Words and Music by Guy Berryman, Jon Buckland, Will Champion and Chris Martin

First note

Verse
Moderately slow

1. Come up to meet _____ you, tell you I'm sor -
2. *See additional lyrics*

- ry, you don't know how love - ly you are. _____ I had to find _

_____ you, tell you I need _____ you, tell you I'll set _____ you a - part. _____

Tell me your se - crets and ask me your ques - tions, oh, let's go back

to the start. _____ Run - ning in cir - cles, com - ing up tails, _

heads on a si - lence a - part. _____

Chorus

No - bod - y said _____ it was eas - y. _____

Oh, it's _____ such a shame _____ for us to part. _____

No - bod - y said _____ it was eas - y. _____

No _____ one ev - er { said _____ it would be this _____ hard. _____
{ said it would be so _____ hard. _____

Oh, take me } back to the start. _____
I'm go - ing }

Additional Lyrics

2. I was just guessing at numbers and figures,
   Pulling the puzzles apart.
   Questions of science, science and progress
   Do not speak as loud as my heart.
   And tell me you love me, come back and haunt me.
   Oh, and I rush to the start.
   Running in circles, chasing tails,
   Coming back as we are.

Southern Cross

Words and Music by Stephen Stills, Richard Curtis and Michael Curtis

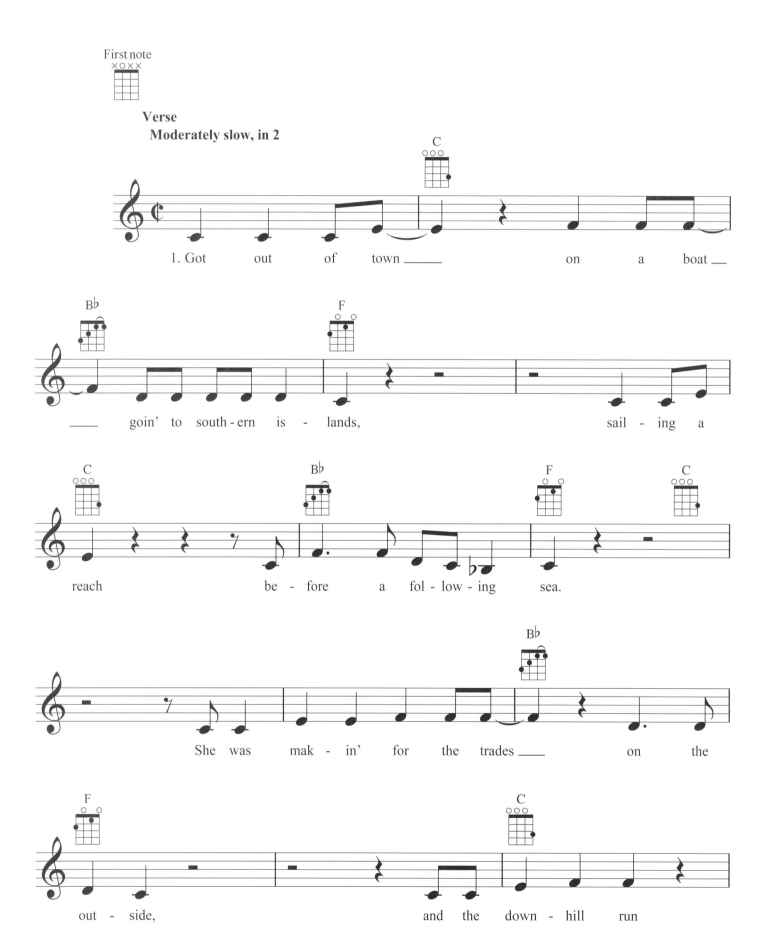

When You Say Nothing at All

Words and Music by Don Schlitz and Paul Overstreet

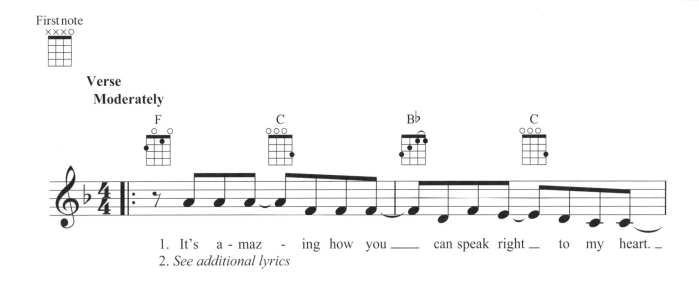

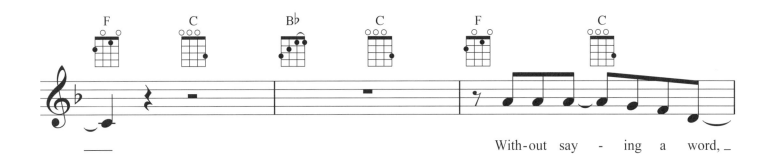

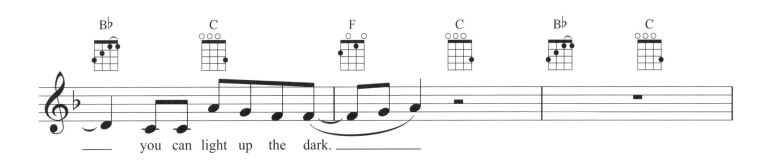

what I hear ___ when you don't ___ say a thing. ___ The

Chorus

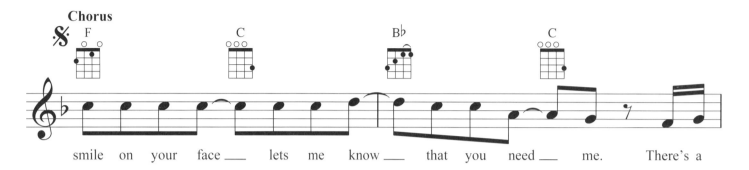

smile on your face ___ lets me know ___ that you need ___ me. There's a

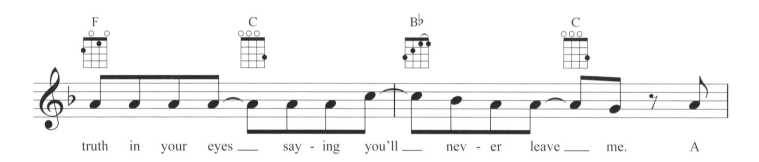

truth in your eyes ___ say - ing you'll ___ nev - er leave ___ me. A

touch of your hand ___ says you'll catch ___ me if ev - er I fall. ___

To Coda ⊕

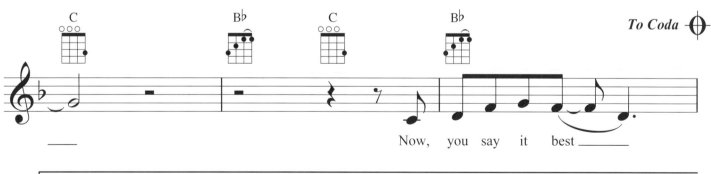

Now, you say it best _____

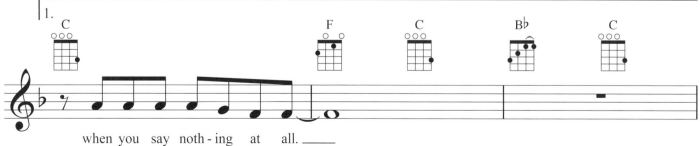

when you say noth - ing at all. ___

118

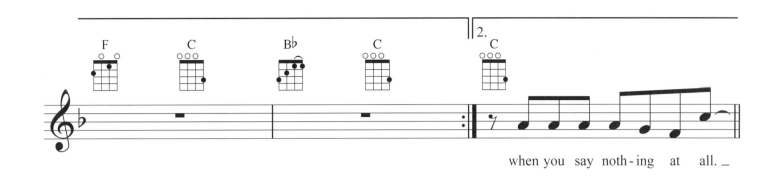

when you say noth-ing at all. _

Interlude

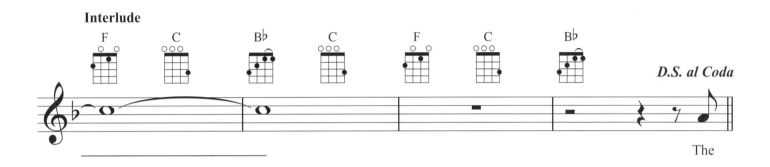

D.S. al Coda

The

Coda

Outro

when you say noth-ing at all. _____

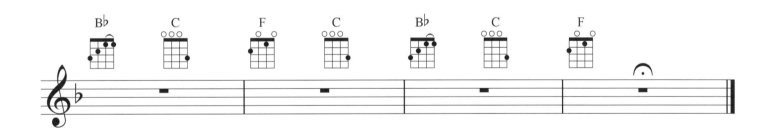

Additional Lyrics

2. All day long I can hear people talking out loud.
   But when you hold me near, you drown out the crowd.
   Old Mister Webster could never define
   What's being said between your heart and mine.

Spanish Harlem

Words and Music by Jerry Leiber and Phil Spector

First note

Verse
Moderately

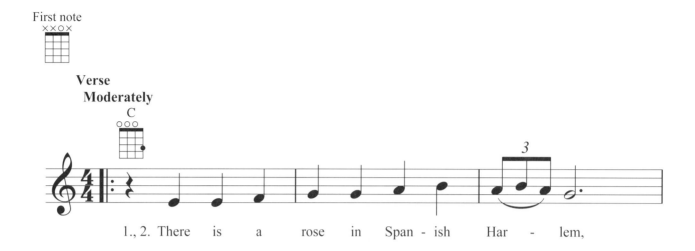

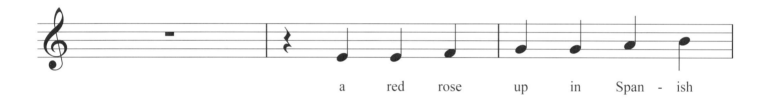

1., 2. There is a rose in Span - ish Har - lem,

a red rose up in Span - ish

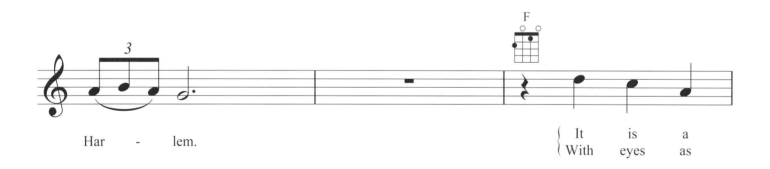

Har - lem.

It is a
With eyes as

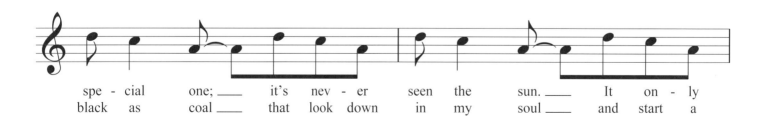

spe - cial one; ___ it's nev - er seen the sun. ___ It on - ly
black as coal ___ that look down in my soul ___ and start a

comes out when the moon is on the run and all the stars are gleam - ing. _____
fire ___ there, and then I lose con - trol. I have to beg your par - don. _____

___   It's grow - ing   in   the   street, _ right up
___   I'm going   to   pick that   rose ___ and watch

through the con - crete, but   soft and   sweet _   and   dream - ing. _____

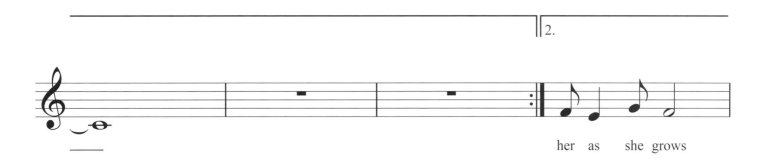

her   as   she grows

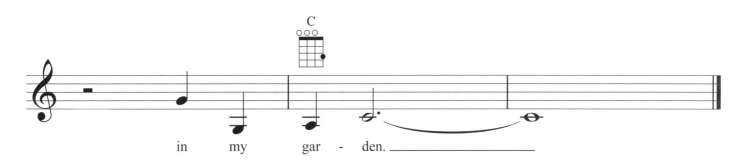

in   my   gar - den. _____

Stay

Words and Music by Mikky Ekko and Justin Parker

First note

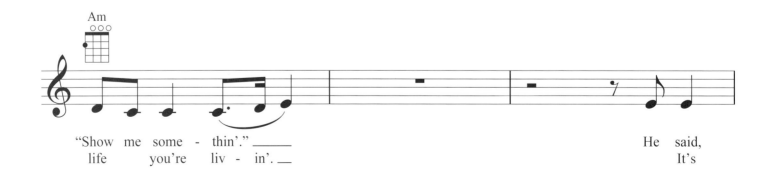

"If you dare, ___ come a lit - tle clos - er."
not just some - thin' you take; it's giv - en.

Pre-Chorus

'Round and a - round and a - round and a - round we go. ___

Oh, ___ now, tell me now, tell me

now, tell me now you know. ___

Chorus

Not real - ly sure how to feel a - bout ___ it. Some - thin' in the way you move ___

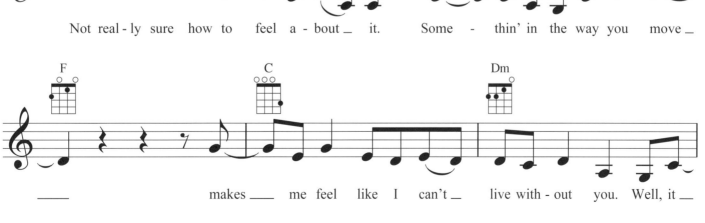

___ makes ___ me feel like I can't ___ live with - out you. Well, it ___

To Coda ⊕

Am   F   C   Dm

_____ takes me all the way. _____ I want you to stay. _____

Am

1.

2.   **Bridge**

F   Am

Ooh, _____ the rea - son I hold _____

Dm   F

_____ on, _____   ooh, _____

Am   Dm

_____ 'cause I need this hole gone. _____

F   Am

Fun - ny you're the bro - ken one but I'm the on - ly one who need - ed sav - in'.

'Cause when you nev - er see the light, it's

D.S. al Coda

hard to know which one of us is cav - in'.

Coda
Outro

Stay.

I want you to stay. ____

Ooh. ____

Steal My Kisses

Words and Music by Ben Harper

First note

1. I pulled in to Nash - ville, Ten - nes - see,   but
2., 3. *See additional lyrics*

you would - n't e - ven come ___ a - round ___ to see   me.   And

since you're head - ing up ___ to Car - o - li - na,   you

know I'm gon - na be right ___ there ___ be - hind ___ ya.   'Cause I

Chorus

al - ways have __ to steal __ my kiss - es from you.

I

al - ways have __ to steal __ my kiss - es from you.

Al - ways have __ to steal __ my kiss - es from ___ you.

I

al - ways have __ to steal __ my kiss - es from __ you. __ 2. Now, I'd ___ you.

3. Now,

Additional Lyrics

2. Now, I'd love to feel that warm southern rain.
   Just to hear it fall is the sweetest sounding thing.
   And to see it fall on your simple country dress,
   It's like heaven to me, I must confess.

3. Now, I've been hanging 'round you for days,
   But when I lean in, you just turn your head away.
   Whoa, no, you didn't mean that.
   She said, "I love the way you think, but I hate the way you act."

A Teenager in Love

Words by Doc Pomus
Music by Mort Shuman

First note

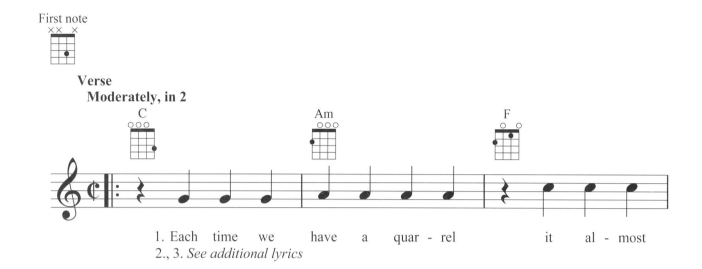

Verse
Moderately, in 2

1. Each time we have a quar - rel it al - most
2., 3. *See additional lyrics*

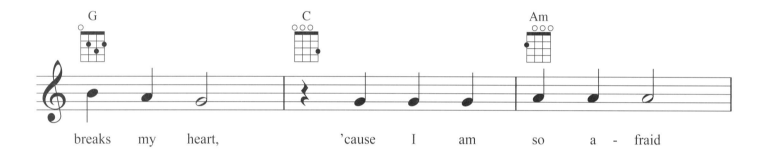

breaks my heart, 'cause I am so a - fraid

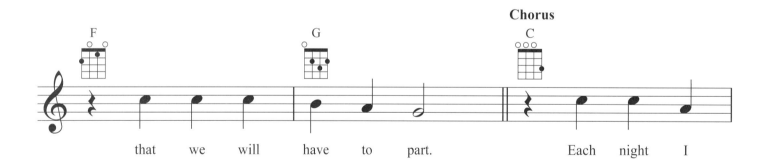

Chorus

that we will have to part. Each night I

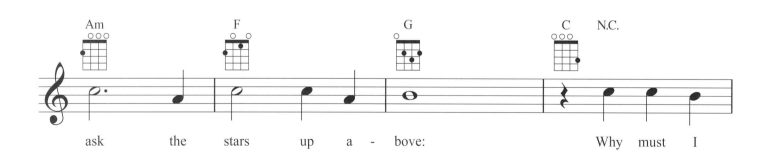

ask the stars up a - bove: Why must I

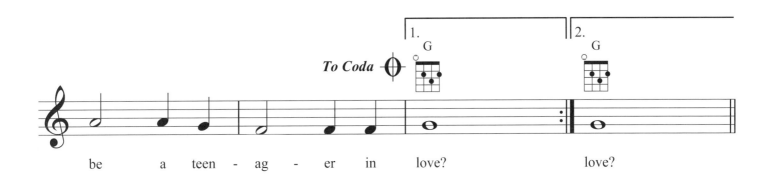

be a teen - ag - er in love? love?

Bridge

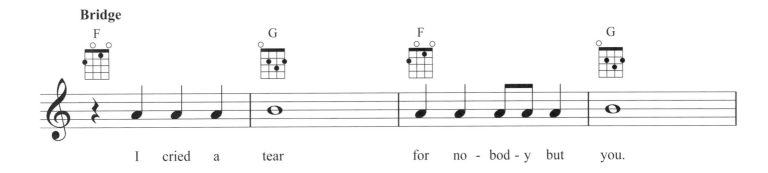

I cried a tear for no - bod - y but you.

D.C. al Coda

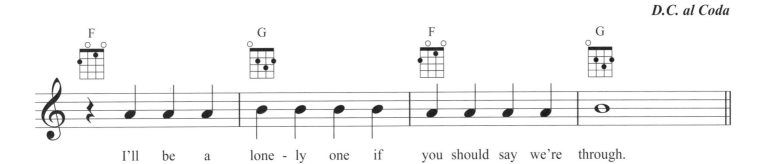

I'll be a lone - ly one if you should say we're through.

Coda

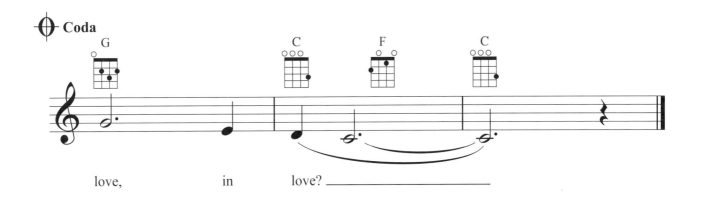

love, in love? _____

Additional Lyrics

2. One day I feel so happy, next day I feel so sad.
   I guess I'll learn to take the good with the bad.

3. If you want to make me cry, that won't be so hard to do.
   And if you should say goodbye, I'll still go on loving you.

The Times They Are A-Changin'

Words and Music by Bob Dylan

First note

Moderately

Verse

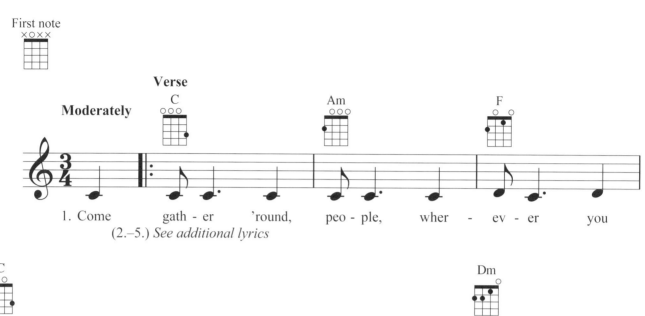

1. Come gath - er 'round, peo - ple, wher - ev - er you

(2.–5.) See additional lyrics

roam, _____ and ad - mit that the wa - ters a -

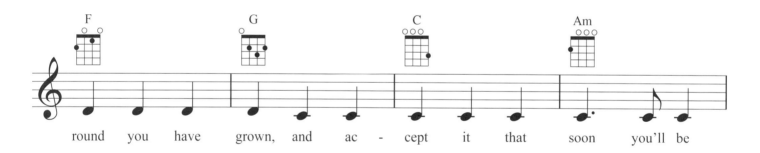

round you have grown, and ac - cept it that soon you'll be

drenched to the bone. _____ If your time to

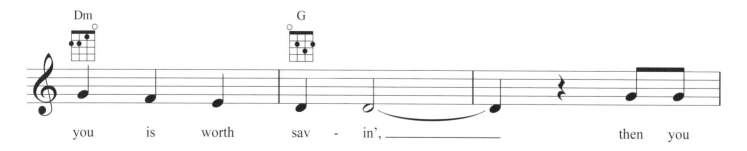

you is worth sav - in', _____ then you

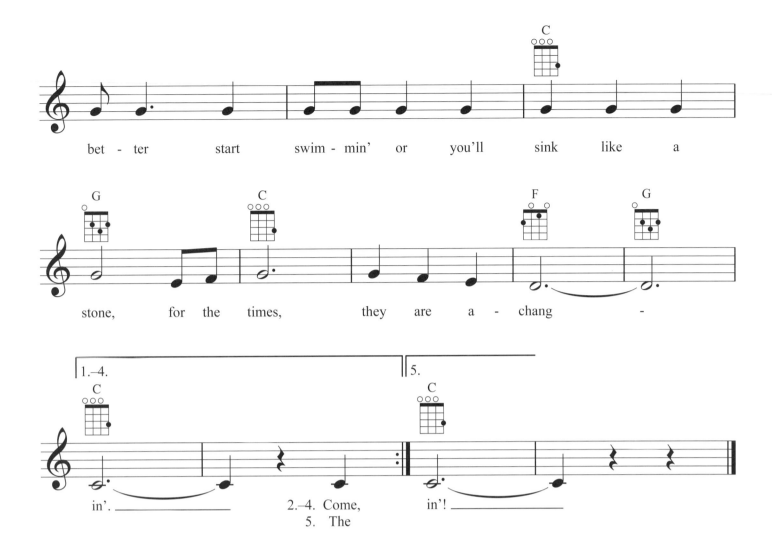

bet - ter   start   swim - min' or   you'll   sink   like   a

stone,   for   the   times,   they   are   a -   chang   -

1.–4.   5.

in'. _____   2.–4. Come,   in'! _____
                              5. The

Additional Lyrics

2. Come, writers and critics who prophesy with your pen,
   And keep your eyes wide; the chance won't come again.
   And don't speak too soon, for the wheel's still in spin,
   And there's no tellin' who that it's namin'.
   For the loser now will be later to win,
   For the times, they are a-changin'.

3. Come, senators, congressmen, please heed the call.
   Don't stand in the doorway, don't block up the hall.
   For he that gets hurt will be he who has stalled.
   There's a battle outside and it's ragin'.
   It'll soon shake your windows and rattle your walls,
   For the times, they are a-changin'!

4. Come, mothers and fathers throughout the land,
   And don't criticize what you can't understand.
   Your sons and your daughters are beyond your command;
   Your old road is rapidly agin'.
   Please get out of the new one if you can't lend your hand,
   For the times, they are a-changin'!

5. The line it is drawn, the curse it is cast.
   The slow one now will later be fast.
   As the present now will later be past,
   The order is rapidly fadin'.
   And the first one now will later be last,
   For the times, they are a-changin'!

Up Around the Bend

Words and Music by John Fogerty

First note

Verse
Moderately

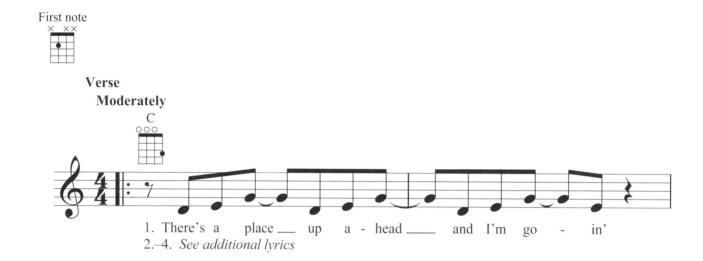

1. There's a place __ up a - head __ and I'm go - in'
2.–4. *See additional lyrics*

just as fast __ as my feet __ can fly. __

Come a - way, __ come a - way, __ if you're go - in',

leave the sink - in' ship __ be - hind. __

Chorus

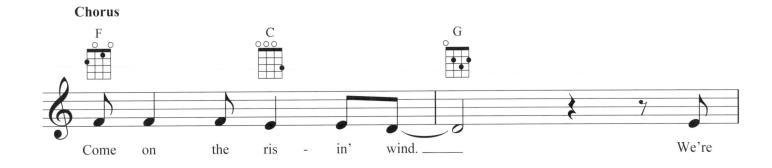

Come on the ris - in' wind. _____ We're

go - in' up ____ a - round the bend, ____ ooh. _____

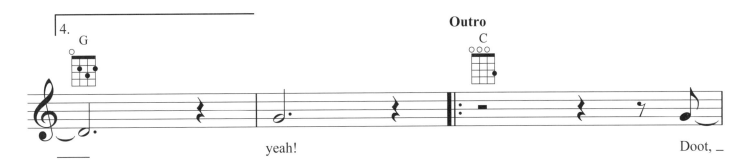

_____ yeah! **Outro** Doot, _

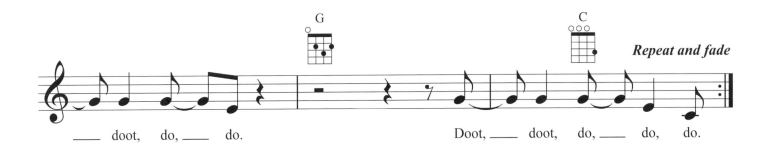

____ doot, do, ____ do. Doot, ____ doot, do, ____ do, do.

Additional Lyrics

2. Bring a song and a smile for the banjo.
   Better get while the gettin's good.
   Hitch a ride to end of the highway
   Where the neons turn to wood.

3. You can ponder perpetual motion,
   Fix your mind on a crystal day.
   Always time for a good conversation,
   There's an ear for what you say.

4. Catch a ride to the end of the highway
   And we'll meet by the big red tree.
   There's a place up ahead and I'm goin'.
   Come along, come along with me.

Time for Me to Fly

Words and Music by Kevin Cronin

You'll Accomp'ny Me

Words and Music by Bob Seger

Originally recorded in E major.

I've seen you smil - ing in the sum - mer sun.
I'll take my chanc - es, babe. I'll risk it all.

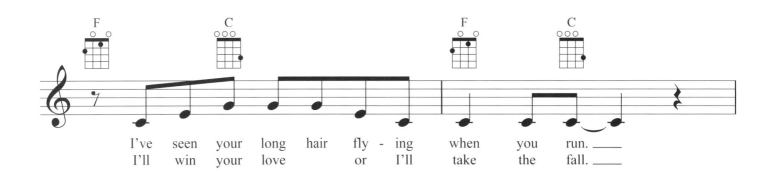

I've seen your long hair fly - ing when you run. ____
I'll win your love or I'll when take the fall. ____

I've made my mind up that it's meant to be.
I've made my mind up, girl. It's meant to be.

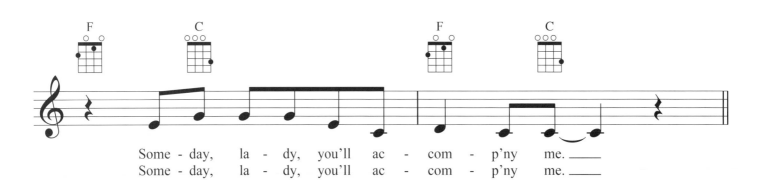

Some - day, la - dy, you'll ac - com - p'ny me. ____
Some - day, la - dy, you'll ac - com - p'ny me. ____

𝄋 Chorus

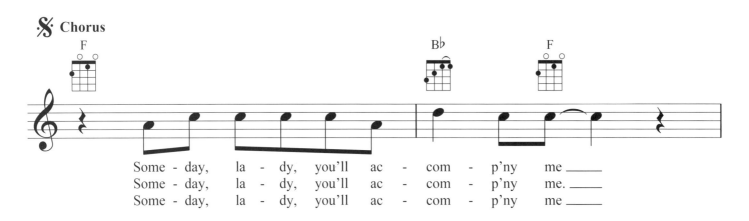

Some - day, la - dy, you'll ac - com - p'ny me ____
Some - day, la - dy, you'll ac - com - p'ny me. ____
Some - day, la - dy, you'll ac - com - p'ny me ____

out where the riv - ers meet the sound - ing sea. ____
It's writ - ten down some - where. It's got ____ to be. ____
out where the riv - ers meet the sound - ing sea. ____

You're high a - bove me now. You're wild and free. ____ Ah, but
You're high a - bove me, fly - ing wild and free. ____ Oh, but
I feel it in my soul. It's meant to be. ____ Oh,

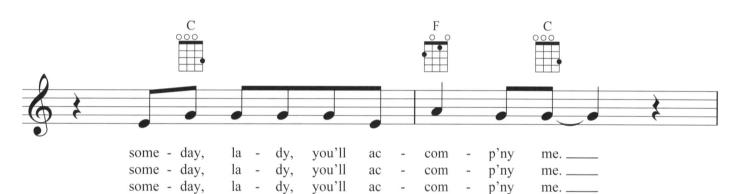

some - day, la - dy, you'll ac - com - p'ny me. ____
some - day, la - dy, you'll ac - com - p'ny me. ____
some - day, la - dy, you'll ac - com - p'ny me. ____

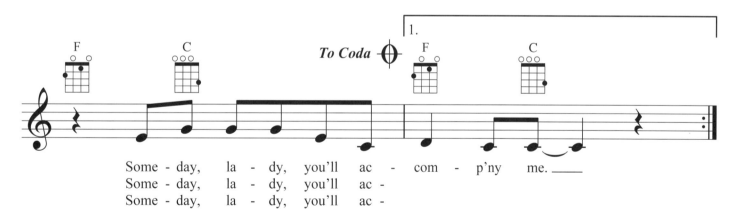

Some - day, la - dy, you'll ac - com - p'ny me. ____
Some - day, la - dy, you'll ac -
Some - day, la - dy, you'll ac -

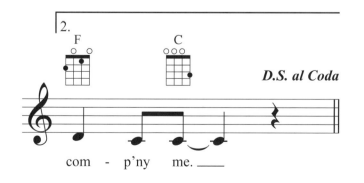

com - p'ny me. ____

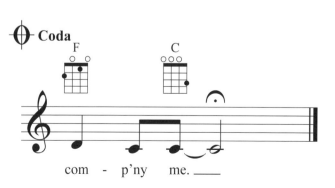

com - p'ny me. ____

Where Have All the Flowers Gone?

Words and Music by Pete Seeger

First note

Verse
Moderately fast

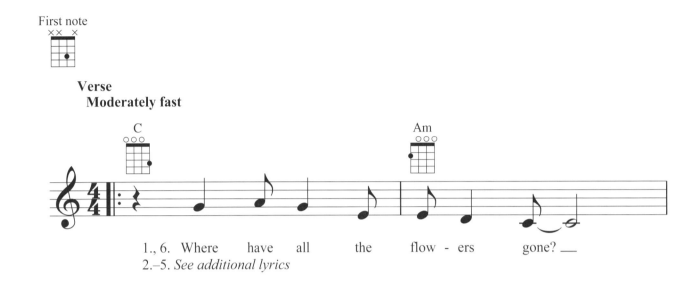

1., 6. Where have all the flow-ers gone? ___
2.–5. *See additional lyrics*

Long time pass - ing. ___ Where have all the

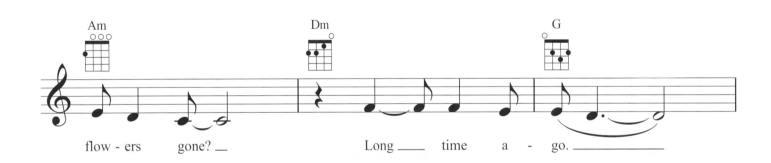

flow-ers gone? ___ Long ___ time a - go. ___

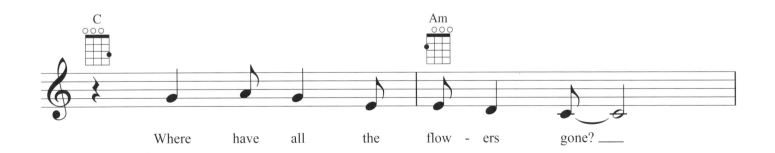

Where have all the flow-ers gone? ___

Additional Lyrics

2. Where have all the young girls gone?
   Long time passing.
   Where have all the young girls gone?
   Long time ago.
   Where have all the young girls gone?
   Gone for husbands, every one.
   Oh, when will they ever learn?
   Oh, when will they ever learn?

3. Where have all the husbands gone?
   Long time passing.
   Where have all the husbands gone?
   Long time ago.
   Where have all the husbands gone?
   Gone for soldiers, every one.
   Oh, when will they ever learn?
   Oh, when will they ever learn?

4. Where have all the soldiers gone?
   Long time passing.
   Where have all the soldiers gone?
   Long time ago.
   Where have all the soldiers gone?
   Gone to graveyards, every one.
   Oh, when will they ever learn?
   Oh, when will they ever learn?

5. Where have all the graveyards gone?
   Long time passing.
   Where have all the graveyards gone?
   Long time ago.
   Where have all the graveyards gone?
   Gone to flowers, every one.
   Oh, when will they ever learn?
   Oh, when will they ever learn?

With or Without You

Words and Music by U2

give your-self a - way. _____ 3. My hands are tied, _

_____ my bod - y bruised. _ You got _ me with _

_____ noth - ing to win _____ and _____ noth - ing left _ to lose. _

And you

With or with - out _____ you, _____

with or with - out you, _ oh. _____ I can't live _

_____ with or with - out _____ you. _____

You Raise Me Up

Words and Music by Brendan Graham and Rolf Lovland

First note

Verse
Moderately slow

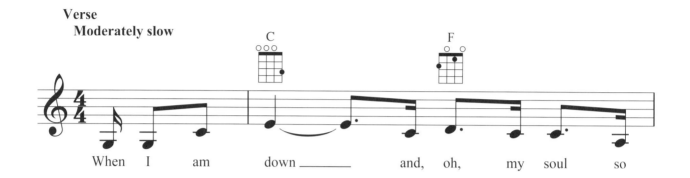

When I am down _____ and, oh, my soul so

wea - ry, when trou - bles come and my heart ___ bur - dened

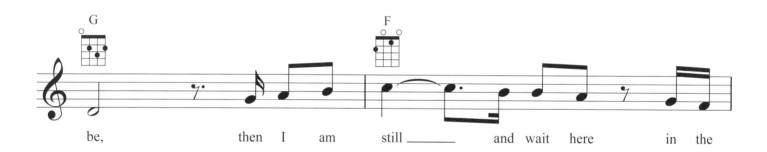

be, then I am still _____ and wait here in the

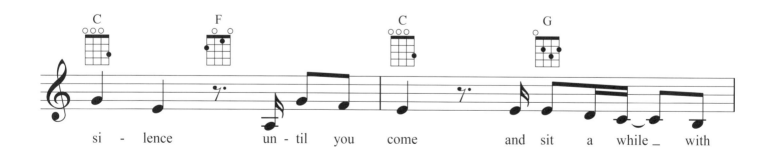

si - lence un - til you come and sit a while ___ with

Chorus

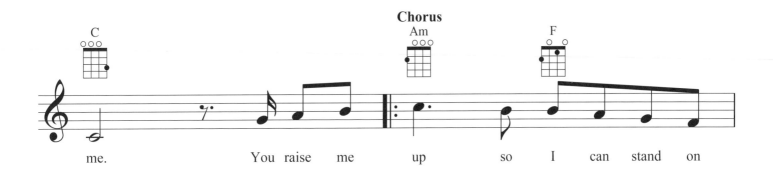

me. You raise me up so I can stand on

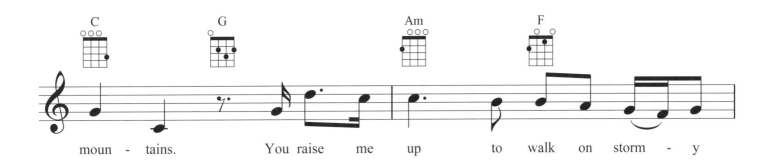

moun - tains. You raise me up to walk on storm - y

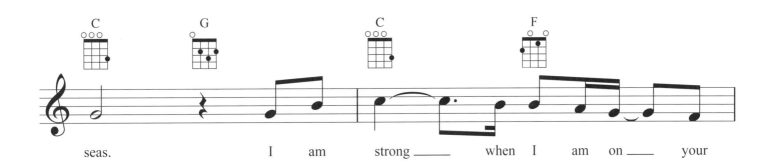

seas. I am strong _____ when I am on _____ your

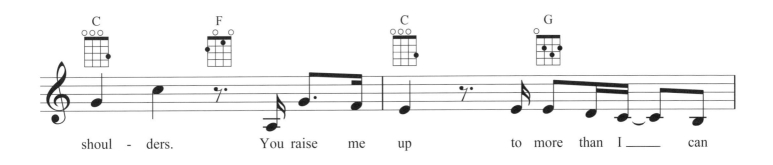

shoul - ders. You raise me up to more than I _____ can

1. be. You raise me 2. be.

Wonderful Tonight

Words and Music by Eric Clapton

First note

Verse
Moderately

1. It's late in the eve - ning;
2. We go to a par - ty,
3. It's time to go home ___ now,

she's won - d'ring what clothes __ to wear. __
ev - 'ry - one turns ___ to see ___
I've got an ach - ing head. __

She puts on her make -
this beau - ti - ful la -
So I give her the car __

- up
- dy
___ keys,

and brush - es her long, ___ blonde hair. __
is walk - ing a - round ___ with me. __
and she helps me to bed. ___

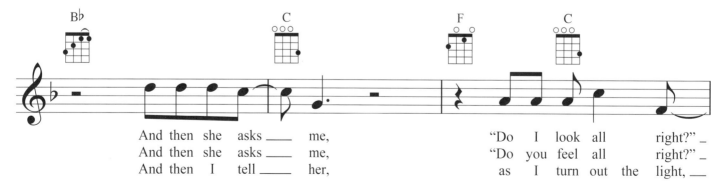

And then she asks ___ me,
And then she asks ___ me,
And then I tell ___ her,

"Do I look all right?" _
"Do you feel all right?" _
as I turn out the light, _

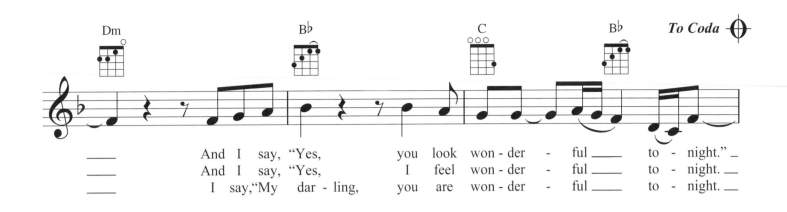

To Coda

And I say, "Yes, you look won - der - ful ___ to - night." _
And I say, "Yes, I feel won - der - ful ___ to - night. _
I say, "My dar - ling, you are won - der - ful ___ to - night. _

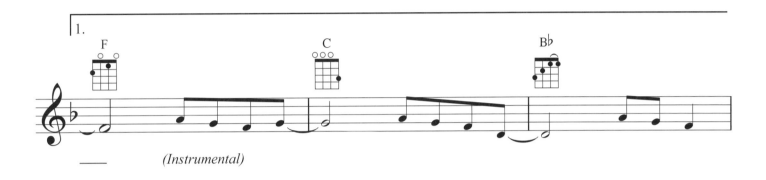

1.

___ *(Instrumental)*

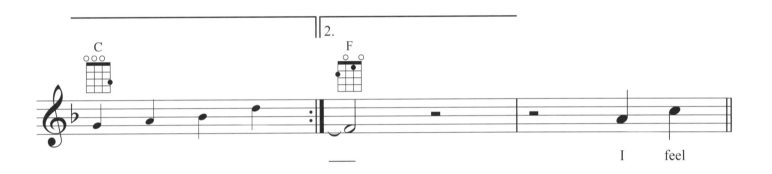

2.

___ I feel

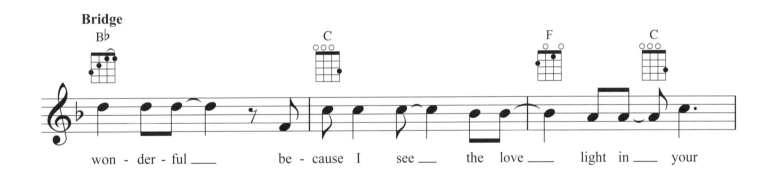

Bridge

won - der - ful ___ be - cause I see ___ the love ___ light in ___ your

eyes. Then the won - der of it all ___ is that you

just don't re - al - ize _____ how much _____ I love _____ you." *(Instrumental)*

D.C. al Coda

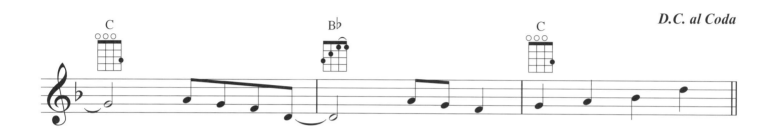

⊕ **Coda**　　　　　　　　　　　　　　　　　　　　**Outro**

_____　　　　　　Oh,　my　dar - ling,　　you　are

won - der - ful _____ to - night." _____　　　(Instrumental)